DEMOCRACY IN WORLD POLITICS

THE STAFFORD LITTLE LECTURES

AT PRINCETON UNIVERSITY, 1955

DEMOCRACY

IN WORLD POLITICS

BY LESTER B. PEARSON

PRINCETON UNIVERSITY PRESS

PRINCETON, NEW JERSEY

1955

PREFACE

I was very greatly honoured, and not a little impressed, by the invitation to give the Stafford Little Lectures, this year of grace and grim anxiety, 1955.

I was impressed because the conclusion that I drew from the invitation, that I still have some claim to membership in the company of scholars, is one that is always agreeable to a person engaged in the practice of politics. I am, of course, not apologetic about my political profession. Indeed, I am proud of a calling which deserves a far better reputation than it has acquired; though, I confess, it could earn an even better reputation than it now deserves. If its repute is relatively low that is due in part to the aspersions cast on it by those who feel such criticism necessary to justify their own non-participation!

For a few years I was an historian. My scholarly apparatus by now is certainly rusty; but I retain as vivid a conviction as ever that, if current opinions and popular prejudices are not to impose themselves with relentless force on our minds, we must judge them in the light of historical knowledge and historical experience, and of the truths that have been tested by such experience. To stand imaginatively for a while in another age is one of the best ways of assessing the problems of the present. It is good also, in the press of business and the restless rush, to renew our acquaintance with those great creations of the human mind and spirit in which there is room to move about, room in which to appreciate the resources that man has within himself.

This satisfaction, indeed this relief, that I get from a return to the atmosphere of scholarship, of intellectual enquiry, is not, I suspect, often shared by scholars who have had the reverse experience by moving into the area, and the smoky atmosphere, of politics. Indeed, experience with politics and politicians often alarms, and has, I suppose, for many thousands of years, those whose approach to their problems is characterized by the serenity and sagacity that comes from exposure to and acquaintance with the enduring.

A former colleague of mine at the University of Toronto, Professor Brebner, put this uneasiness of the scholar at the activities of the politician in polite but understandable terms in his address on Humility (a good subject for anyone, and especially for public servants) at the third Columbia University bicentennial convocation in November 1954. He said then: "It is the agglomeration of physical power, social power, economic power, and propagandistic power as the . . . prize for which artists in political power contend that most alarms the community of scholars. For politics is an art of the immediate, and statesmanship which rests on longer, deeper views, is rare."

It is because in these lectures I have to try to take the "longer, deeper view" that my pleasure in being at Princeton is not unmixed with anxiety lest I shall not be able to do justice to the occasion; or prove a worthy successor to the long and distinguished list of Stafford Little lecturers that preceded me.

I have recently been looking at that list and I was greatly impressed, not only by the names of so many men of real distinction, but by the catholicity, the far-reaching range of the subjects they discussed.

How I would have liked to listen to Oliver St. John Gogarty on "Incredible Culture"; or Lin Yutang on "The Reasonable Spirit"! It must have been reasonable in that year of the middle thirties, because in the succeeding one you were able to listen to a Professor from Moscow! There was another lecture in the same year, by William Beebe, the title of which reminded me of the way I feel occasionally when I wrestle with some international problems. It was called "Four hundred fathoms down"!

There were other subjects discussed here in this series fifteen or twenty years ago, which point up the continuity of our problems and the persistence of our preoccupations: "Expansion of Arab Nationalism," "Crisis in the Far East," "The Social Implications of Science," "Congress and Foreign Policy." It all has a currently familiar ring. There was also in 1935 a lecture by Mr. John Foster Dulles on "Peaceful Change Within the Society of Nations" which I certainly must read!

As I myself am to talk about "Democracy in World Politics" (an omnibus title which gives me, and was meant to, lots of scope), I was more than normally interested to learn that the late Mr. Henry Stimson and eight other Stafford Little lecturers .

have in recent years dealt with various aspects of democracy. It never ceases to be a topical, or a complicated subject. Yet one almost hesitates to mention it now. Its coinage has been so grossly debased since it has been taken over—as a word—by those totalitarians who have betrayed its meaning. Only insult has been added to the injury when they put "popular" in front of it.

I have never been able to find or fashion a definition of democracy that satisfies me. I have read and listened to a lot that do not; slogan definitions or shallow generalizations.

However democracy may be defined, we feel its true meaning deep inside us even when we cannot express it. However good it may be for social and political progress it can only be kept strong and healthy by honest and intelligent individual judgment and action. That is not easy today in the confusion of voices which press on us from the world in which we live, a confusion which is itself often mistaken for democracy. But easy or not, democracy must be kept strong—with a strength that is not only military and economic, but also intellectual and moral.

LESTER B. PEARSON

Ottawa
May 7, 1955

CONTENTS

Preface   v

I. Old Problems on a New Scale   3

II. Proportions of Force   9

III. Coalitions: the New Units of Policy   40

IV. Open Diplomacy: Negotiating
    in the Spotlight   55

V. Open Diplomacy: The United Nations   64

VI. Relations between Civilizations   82

VII. Democracy and the Power of Decision   96

ix

DEMOCRACY IN WORLD POLITICS

CHAPTER I

OLD PROBLEMS ON A NEW SCALE

During the past fifty years, liberal and representative democracy has found itself in grave and at times nearly mortal jeopardy. There is reason to think that the challenges which lie ahead of us may be quite as difficult to meet as those which we have already faced in the first half of what Sir Winston Churchill has called the "terrible twentieth century."

Most of these challenges are, however, distinguished chiefly by the gigantic new scale in which they present themselves. Often they are the same old problems, now "writ large."

The size of contemporary problems is apt to make them appear overwhelming, but they need not prove so. In world politics, as in such varied other fields as music or the other arts, mathematics or engineering, mere scale in itself is usually of secondary importance. The fundamentals relate rather to questions of values or proportion. Quantity itself is relative. In an increase in size, the new factors often prove on examination to break down into elements that make familiar if difficult demands on us. So it is foolish to let mere size daunt us; even if at times the quantitative change becomes so great as to produce something that seems entirely new.

Though the scale of our political problems has increased, and the stakes have mounted so high that they may involve survival for the human race, the essential character of those problems is not new. Men have faced them before, though whether this is comforting or not is open to question. They have been successfully resolved more than once, but there have been failures too. Now, however, the penalty for failure—or for serious blundering—is far greater than ever before. Mankind can no longer afford much blundering.

Many of our difficulties and dangers today are in substantial part the result of past failures. Paradoxically, there are others which are largely the result of successes; especially our successes in the fields of natural science and technology.

It is one of the characteristics of life, for societies as well as for individuals, that the consequence of success in grappling with problems is often the opportunity and the obligation to meet and master greater ones. We are forever climbing the ever mounting slope.

We are most likely to climb successfully, and to reach our objective, if we have acquired some criteria that bear on, and some clues to the nature and meaning of past experience. This will help us to take the measure of difficult situations which we are bound to meet and to reach the right decisions on which so much will depend.

Two such criteria have, I suggest, been central to Western civilization through the whole of its history.

The first is the individual man as the focus of aspiration and action. A Greek philosopher, Protagoras, expressed this some 2400 years ago in the aphorism that "man is the measure of all things." This begs a more fundamental question, but so far as it goes, Protagoras' assertion is true, and it has proved one of the great liberating insights and impulses of history. Many of the achievements of Greek thought and art are monuments to this view. In more recent times the Renaissance, the humanist movements, and the development of Parliamentary democracy may be counted as essays in working out the implications of its basic vision.

The other criterion which has been central to our civilization deals with the consequential but more searching question, "What is the measure of man?" This leads to the recognition that although man is indeed the measure of all other things, there is also a measure for him, for the individual human being, against which he can be tested. That measure is to be found in values that, while fully human, are at the same time both universal and absolute; that are, in short, moral and spiritual.

The aspirations and values of the men who have shaped our civilization have, of course, been varied in the extreme. But they have been linked by a common thread, the inspiration that comes from some vision of this two-fold pattern.

Though they naturally do not in themselves offer any simple rule of thumb for dealing with the challenges that may come, these criteria do, I suggest, offer us help in responding to them, as well as a mo-

5

tive for the efforts which we will have to make if we are to do this successfully.

One aspect of our problems which, in nature if not in scope, is not new, is that the objective, the long-term purpose in international politics, remains for men of goodwill what it has always been—so to act, in response to the demands of neighbourhood, as to encourage the growth of neighbourliness, of friendship.

All men do not, of course, seek these objectives. All men never have. There are those who prefer conflict to cooperation, power to peace. Some say it will always be so and politics and society can never be based on any other assumption. In this matter, however, I am on the side of the angels. I believe that there is a higher proportion of men of good-will in the world today than ever before, and that the dazzling technical and scientific developments of our age may be accompanied by an increase, rather than a decrease in that number.

Erich Fromm, in his book *The Fear of Freedom,* expresses this optimistic viewpoint in the following words:

"There is no reason to wonder why the record of history shows so much cruelty and distructiveness. If there is anything to be surprised at—and encouraged by—I believe it is the fact that the human race in spite of all that has happened to men has retained—and actually developed—such qualities of dignity, courage, decency and kindness as

we find in them throughout history and in count-
less individuals today."

Neighbourhood has always been measured in
terms of the distance over which men and ideas and
things can be readily and rapidly transported. One
of the results of the amazing material developments
of our age is that, for some purposes at least, neighbourhood has now become a fact on a global scale.
That is an alteration in scale which we have to take
into account in world politics. Unfortunately, we have
yet to match this inescapable fact with a corresponding achievement on any such scale in the area, and
the depth, of neighbourliness and friendship.

We have, I think, solved this problem on this continent, and both our peoples are rightly proud of this
achievement. We need, however, the application—
on a far wider front—of that concept of neighbourliness and cooperation which characterizes the relations between the United States and Canada. Some
progress has been made. The development of security by collective action, and of technical assistance
and economic aid to the underdeveloped countries,
show that we have already begun to move in the
right direction. We will, however, have to go further;
and this is going to be even more difficult.

The stepped-up scale on which our generation has
to face the problems of human relationships—which
is what politics is—is seen in a number of areas. One
is the quantity of power available to men as an instrument of policy; another is the size of the political

societies which have to formulate policies. The major problems of diplomacy today are no longer between national states but between civilizations; some indeed are common to mankind as a whole. Within democratic societies, too, the number of those who take an interest in, and who influence, the decisions which shape the future, is incomparably greater than ever before in history.

What follows is an attempt to examine something of what this new order of magnitude means in relation to democracy and world politics.

CHAPTER II

PROPORTIONS OF FORCE

One problem which presents itself to our generation on a new and vastly enlarged scale arises out of new facts of force. Nuclear science has now placed in the hands of some men and governments, and will soon place in the hands of many others, destructive force on a scale which by any previous standards is fantastic.

This stepping-up of the quantity of force available for use as an instrument of the policy of nations underlines and lends particular urgency to problems in other and related fields.

Few men in or out of governments have, I suspect, been able to appreciate the implications for democracy and world politics of the discovery of this new physical power that men have learned to set off, but not yet to subdue. But it does not take any unusual insight to recognize that certain ideals of human and political behaviour, the achievement of which has hitherto been considered desirable if humanity is to live peacefully and well, may within the near future become essential if humanity is to live at all. We will henceforth have to take far more seriously a number of things which, until now, men have been able to ignore, if not with impunity, at least without immediately disastrous results.

Since the beginning of history, each individual man and woman has had the capacity for suicide. As individuals, we have learned to live with this capacity; almost to ignore it. We have now reached that stage in history when what has always been true on the individual and spiritual level has become true also on a world-wide social and political plane. To survive, we must accept and put into practice the organizational or political implications of these facts. The first step in doing so is clearly to realize the dimensions of the situation, and then to act on that realization through policies which will often have to be supra-national in inspiration and result.

It is hard enough to grasp even the basic technical facts which threaten to bring about this revolution in what I might call the imperatives of international ethics. Until a few years ago the most powerful weapon ever used was, I suppose, a bomb containing ten tons of TNT explosive. The atom bomb dropped at Hiroshima had the equivalent of 20,000 tons of TNT. In other words, the increase was of the order of a thousand-fold. The large so-called hydrogen weapons presently available have increased this scale still another thousand-fold, so that they are now measured in megatons, a unit of explosion a million times greater than that used in World War II.

Today the difference between the big megaton fusion weapon and the standard atomic fission weapon is quite as great as the difference between the fission weapon and what we now, with a sad if unconscious irony, call the "conventional" bombs of

World War II. We are dealing now not with two orders of magnitude in destruction, but with three. Is this the end? Thirty-five years ago, the Rt. Hon. Herbert Asquith said that science had just then begun to "lisp the alphabet of annihilation." Has she even now said her last word?

The power of these hydrogen explosives, in terms of blast, is startling enough. But a much more serious feature of this power is that a burst of a single bomb can pollute with radioactive poison, or "fallout" as it is called, thousands of square miles.

Quite apart from the destructive effect of blast and local fall-out, it is conceivable that the explosion, within a fairly short period, of a few hundred hydrogen weapons or appropriately cased fission weapons, anywhere in the world, might so contaminate the atmosphere as to threaten grave and lingering illness to many millions of the earth's inhabitants—and that the use of a few thousand such explosives anywhere might threaten the existence of all human life.

Furthermore, and this is often forgotten in discussions of this matter, within our present generation not merely the United States, the U.S.S.R. and the United Kingdom, but several other countries may have the power to manufacture and to deliver nuclear explosives to any target.

It is vitally important that we try to think through the political and defence implications of force problems of such horrible magnitude, and reexamine various assumptions which we have accepted concerning this whole matter.

For some this reexamination has led to the thesis that the terrific destructive power of these weapons may itself make a major war less likely, or even impossible. Instead of destroying humanity, it may destroy war. If each side has the capacity utterly to destroy the other, and if each side's retaliatory capacity is sufficiently dispersed and protected that no aggressor could hope to knock it out before retaliation was launched, then the results of beginning a war would be known in advance to be mutual destruction. Provided paralysis of the will is avoided, and known to be avoided, then against rational and informed men such a deterrent should be effective. It would not stop a bad and mad man—a Hitler—but it would stop one who was merely bad. So runs the thesis.

Some time ago, even Mr. Malenkov was reported to have admitted in various speeches that another war would be the end of world civilization. For this he was reproved by *Pravda,* and Russian propagandists now pretend again that communist society could survive such a war, that only capitalism would collapse. There is always a danger that men may eventually believe their own propaganda by a process of auto-intoxication, but I think it unlikely that the Russian dictators in the Kremlin are really so naive or ill-informed. We know that physically, if not politically, they are with us in this hydrogen world; that we do, in a very real sense, "co-exist." I hope and believe that they know it too. Such realization may make for agreement on the basis, if not of a common regard, at least of a common fear.

There is perhaps more danger that the Chinese Communist leaders (still in the flush of revolutionary victory and possessed of nationalist and communist messianic delusions) may have convinced themselves that they will enjoy sufficient immunity from the consequences of nuclear war to ensure the continuance of their national power and political organization. They are reported to cherish the view that China has so many people, and a society so undeveloped, so uncomplicated, so elastic, as to be relatively secure against any cataclysm. China could "roll" with even a nuclear punch and never be knocked out. Though in a war they might lose a hundred million men or more, they would have five hundred million left and could survive; whereas Western countries could not.

This comforting illusion, however, may be modified by the knowledge that, as Sir Winston Churchill and others have noted, the hydrogen bomb is a great equalizer of numbers, and a great neutralizer of geography, to a far greater extent than previous weapons. These weapons operate against areas rather than armies, make continents vulnerable as well as countries. Each one can make thousands of square miles an uninhabited desolation, however heavily or sparsely populated it may have been. They give a new twist to geopolitics and demand a new approach to military and diplomatic strategy.

In this situation it is, I think, very foolish and no service to peace or security for either side in the cold war to hurl threats and bravados against the other. Rattling hydrogen atoms is as infantile as rattling sabres but far more dangerous. Hydrogen and hate is a bad mixture. With the stakes so high, it is now more necessary than ever for political and military leaders to keep hot blood from overruling good sense, to think quietly before acting or talking wildly.

Many people in the West think of communist leaders as coldly calculating men, chess players with icy self-control. No doubt some are. But temper, passion, self-righteous indignation, and the emotional outbursts which can come from prolonged frustration, can be part of their political and emotional equipment as well. The danger that totalitarian despots may take passionate gambles with new power is therefore always with us. So is that which may result from defensive-preventive moves by democracies who have come to the end of patience and restraint, who have been driven by their increasing fears into unwise policies which might have unintended but unhappy results.

There is danger also from another source.

At present there are governments in the Far East whose leaders have an interest in involving others in their wars, as the only way in which certain national policies can be achieved. Their ultimate goals may themselves be worthy ones with which we may sympathize, however much we disagree with the methods proposed for their achievement: goals which

14

concern the recovery of freedom and national territory lost to Communists. To reach them may seem to require a renewal of hostilities in which, these leaders assume, certain nations of the West would be on their side. Though the Asian governments concerned may themselves leave something to be desired in their practice of democracy or in their devotion to the liberty of the citizen, such a war of "liberation" is always proclaimed as a struggle for democracy, on the assumption, doubtless, that anything that is anti-communist is democratic. According to this theory, Hitler would be the greatest of all democrats, a proposition that may be questioned!

When the time comes that nuclear weapons are more widely held among states, this danger will increase. When pressures of the kind I have just described become too much for men or governments with effective sovereignty over a certain area and certain forces, or even effective control for a short period over a few nuclear weapons, the results might be, to say the least, unfortunate.

Such an international dispersal of these new weapons would also affect the current theory of the nuclear deterrent, of massive retaliation. In certain situations today, this may be our best hope for safety. Nevertheless it is based, among other things, on an assumption of bi-polarity in the world, which is already an over-simplification and may, before long, be overtaken by events.

If we ever reach the nightmare stage where each of a dozen or so countries has a stock of hydrogen weapons, with intercontinental missiles and launching sites in each one aimed at the heart of a good selection of the others, just how would multilateral deterrents operate then?

All this suggests that the doctrine of massive retaliation and the nuclear deterrent, to which I subscribe as *one* element, but only one, in a sound foreign and defence policy, is far from ideal. It seems at best to provide a short-term method of gaining time, rather than a long-term solution of the problem of peace.

It is also worth reminding ourselves of the effect of the possession of nuclear weapons and the ability to wage nuclear warfare, on the theory and practice of national sovereignty. You will remember that John Stuart Mill, a century ago, drew a distinction in his famous *Essay on Liberty* between what could be called "self-regarding" and "other-regarding" actions. This, in his system of ethics, was a basis for the maintenance of individual freedom consistent with the protection of society. It may be that some such modification of the theory of sovereignty will have to be added to those which we have already accepted in the interests of our own security. On the international plane it is unlikely that rational men, however devoted to the principle of national self-determination, will continue indefinitely to believe in any theory of sovereignty that would make it legally possible for an irresponsible small nation to devote its economic resources to building up a stockpile of long-range ballistic missiles with hydro-gen warheads, and launching sites aimed at its neighbours anywhere on the globe.

These problems are still, of course, years ahead. It may seem idle to worry about them now. They are, however, far from academic and deserve the most earnest and informed consideration. Too often it is only the problem of today, or at the best, of tomorrow, which commands public attention and pro-vokes discussion.

There is one problem, however, that could face us either today or tomorrow. It arises from the widely held but mistaken view that all nuclear weapons are in the same category of destructive force and that none are therefore likely to be used except in an all-out world war, that small wars are somehow differ-ent, not so dangerous, and can be isolated without too much difficulty.

This might be a reasonable thesis if there were only large nuclear fusion weapons, the equivalent of hundreds of thousands or even millions of tons of TNT. It is possible that such horror weapons of mass destruction would not be used in any war, ex-cept in one of desperation and extermination. To avoid such a general calamity, there might develop a tacit acceptance on both sides of a self-denying ordinance against hydrogen strategic bombing of any kind in any war because of the mutual destruc-tion and chaos which might ensue.

Now, however, small atomic weapons, with explosive power amounting to only a few per cent of the large mass-destruction nuclear weapons are common. This creates a new situation.

President Eisenhower said on March 16, 1955: "Now in any combat where these things [smaller nuclear weapons] can be used against strictly military targets and for strictly military purposes, I see no reason why they should not be used just exactly as you would use a bullet or anything else." It may be unrealistic, therefore, to assume that these smaller tactical weapons will not be used if there are hostilities, local *or* general.

To obtain the same military results from conventional weapons in such tasks as neutralizing airfields or lines of communication, fifty or a hundred times as many bombs and aeroplanes and pilots would be required, but with no less destruction. Furthermore, if the new atomic weapons could not be used for every possible tactical purpose, the advantage in the hands of those with overwhelmingly more manpower and with cynical ruthlessness in its use, could in some situations be decisive.

If, therefore, we are indeed entering a period where it would be wrong to expect that atomic weapons in some form will not be used in the event of hostilities, large or small, by those powers that possess them, certain conclusions follow which should be carefully examined.

The first, of course, is that it is more essential than ever to avoid by every possible and honourable means hostilities of any kind. A war which begins on an island may soon spread to a world. The use by one side of tactical A-bombs against a military establishment may, under the dread and ruthless momentum of fear, hate, and destruction, lead to strategic H-bombs against a metropolis.

I do not mean that the free peoples should always retreat in the face of danger, or of threats. Such withdrawals by one side, in which the vacuum is filled by a corresponding advance by the other, even though they may be at times wise and necessary, are often no contribution to real peace. The result may be too easily and too often an unfounded expectation by the advancing side of still further withdrawals by the other, and a heightened anger and frustration, rising too close to the exploding point, by the side which has made the concession.

When withdrawals are necessary and wise, they must therefore be followed by other moves to avoid conflict and to remove its causes. There are such things as the neutralized zone or buffer, which has been tried out by land in Korea, and might perhaps usefully be attempted elsewhere on land or water. There are cease-fire, truce and stand-still arrangements, and agreements not to use force in a given situation.

Wise men should not scorn devices or expedients of this kind which can gain time for more fundamental solutions to mature, and which may avoid a war which is unlikely to be kept "conventional" and which could quickly spread across oceans and continents.

While such temporary measures may often be required, these should not distract us from the vital and continuous search for fundamental solutions. In this search we should not forget that the danger is not technical, but political. It comes not from the discovery of processes which set off the fission or fusion of atoms with unprecedented explosive power, but from the fact that these processes are now in the hands of men who have for centuries been using force against each other.

We should, therefore, be careful not to concentrate our time, our energies, and our planning exclusively on the tactics and strategy of defence against and counter-attack by new weapons, to the point that we delay or prejudice the more important task of making their use unlikely by solving international problems and easing international tensions.

The goal still remains the ending of war before it ends us, the search for agreement with those whom we have the most cause to fear, the beating of swords into ploughshares. So we must continue the hard and often seemingly hopeless task of trying to convince those who have made a creed of violence, that now at last violence cannot possibly pay because its end result will be universal destruction.

It may seem unrealistic to the point of phantasy to place the hope for human survival on the achievement of universal non-violence. There is, however, no reason for not trying to move at once toward less reliance on violence rather than more, and also toward reliance on less violence rather than on more.

There is plenty of room for progress in both these directions.

It is the hope of all of us that no atomic weapons will ever have to be used, and that all governments will recognize that the practice of pursuing political objectives against other governments by means of this or any other kind of violence is not only too uncivilized, but too dangerous, to be tolerated any longer in the modern world. Yet the future of civilization, and perhaps of the human race, can hardly be allowed to depend entirely on reaching at once this final goal of self-restraint.

We should therefore try also to develop, if we can, a doctrine of proportion, and do our best to impose it on the other side by the cold logic of fact. If force is used against you, that does not necessarily justify using more in retaliation than is needed for the purpose. You might call this, if you like, the doctrine of "reasonable or measured retaliation." Like "massive retaliation," it is not the whole solution to the problem of aggression and nuclear power, but it is another element in that solution.

In this sense, the measure of force is as important as its nature. There is, it seems to me, danger in the growing tendency of public opinion throughout the world to accept uncritically what may be called the mystique of the atom, as if it were the source of the force that matters rather than its employment and the amount let loose.

I realize, of course, that there are special situations where the kind of force used is of paramount importance. I know perfectly well, for instance, that no amount of logical or technical or philosophical argument would remove the impression in the minds of millions of men that a special horror had been perpetrated on a special race of people who were not white if for the second time anything—however small—which could be labelled an atom bomb, were dropped on an Asian target, and on Asians.

That reaction should be, of course, a very important and possibly a decisive factor in any decision to use or not to use any atomic weapon in a given situation and at a given place. But there is a danger for the future in any generalization of this reasoning, though it may certainly be valid in certain circumstances and in certain areas today.

We hope that atomic weapons will never be used. We also hope that machine-guns and howitzers will not be used. The danger, I suggest, is that the uncritical acceptance throughout the world of the reprehensible quality of atomic weapons as such rather than of violence itself, may lead to an assumption that the use of "conventional" weapons to kill men in order to achieve political objectives is somehow not so objectionable. A man is equally dead if killed by a bullet, an arrow, or an atomic blast. It is the use of force that is to be condemned, not the physical source of that force.

There are differences, naturally, between sending a hundred planes to drop a hundred ten-ton conventional bombs on an airfield, and sending one plane to drop one atomic weapon of the same kiloton explosive power. But the differences are technical, or psychological or even political. They are not moral.

On the other hand, the use of any type of weapon against an airfield, a military camp, or a warship, except in circumstances which clearly imply the launching of a general war of aggression, could not conceivably be held by reasonable men to justify dropping in retaliation a single hydrogen bomb, with the explosive power of a million tons of TNT, on a crowded city of the attacker or his allies. This seems to me to have a direct bearing on that doctrine of "massive retaliation" which I have already mentioned.

It is important, therefore, to reexamine some loose thinking, and loose talk, that has occurred about this doctrine and about the theory of the deterrent. The capacity for massive retaliation and the unambiguous and declared resolve in certain circumstances to use that capacity is, it seems to me, a necessary deterrent against the possibility that a potential aggressor might yield to the temptation of launching an aggressive sudden all-out attack in the hope of quick and final victory. But any idea that such capacity for massive retaliation should or would be used by our side in retaliation against a local attack or conflict, or as a defence against an attack which may not be massive, is something else. The acceptance of such a theory could mean that the very future of the world would hang on the decision whether to reply to a threat against a big warship or a small island by an H-bomb attack on a continent.

There is something very frightening about the idea of playing "all or nothing" with any kind of weapon. In an era where two sides possess thermo-nuclear weapons, the application of the theory of the maximum deterrent for other than the maximum attack might be fatal to both sides.

Indeed, I suggest that such a theory has always been indefensible. Consider the old doctrine of "an eye for an eye, and a tooth for a tooth." In relations with individuals, that doctrine is now generally regarded, in the Western world at least, as primitive and barbarous. So it is, from the viewpoint of *higher* moral standards. But it is well not to forget that there are also *lower* levels, more primitive and more barbarous than that doctrine of equivalents. The theory of the disproportionately heavy deterrent has seldom, in relations with individuals, worked effectively to accomplish any good end. The practice of hanging a man for stealing a sheep is one such lower level which was reached, and which people tried to justify by talk of its deterrent value, more than thirty centuries after the doctrine of proportionate limits to forceful retaliation was propounded by Moses. Happily, men have again risen above that practice in civilized domestic society.

The doctrine that only a limited use of force, proportionate to the circumstances and strictly necessary to accomplish specific objectives, can be justified as self-defence is, I think, inherent in the principles of natural law. Certainly it is basic to the domestic law of all civilized peoples.

In the law of my own country, for example, the principle was expressed by Mr. Justice Martin of the Saskatchewan Court of Appeal in the case of Mac-Neill and Hill: [1]

"While the law recognizes the right of self-defence, the right to repel force with force, no right is to be abused, and the right of self-defence is one which may easily be abused. The force employed must not be out of proportion to the apparent urgency of the occasion."

As Section 66 of the Canadian Criminal Code puts it:

"Everyone authorized by law to use force is criminally responsible for any excess according to the nature and quality of the act which constitutes the excess."

An example of this same principle, chosen from United States law, is found in a case known as *State vs. Cephus,* cited by Wharton, in the following words: [2]

"In repelling or resisting an assault, no more force may be used than is necessary for the purpose, and if the person assaulted uses in his defence greater force than is necessary for the purpose, he becomes the aggressor . . ."

---

[1] II D.L.R. 296—1929.
[2] 67 ATL. 150.
610 PENN. (DEL.) 160.

In English law too the principle exists. Thus Halsbury's *Laws of England,* on page 448, reads:

"A person lawfully defending himself or his habitation is not bound to retreat or to give way to the aggressor before killing him: he is even entitled to follow him and to endeavour to capture him; but if the aggressor is captured or is retreating without offering resistance and is then killed the person killing him is guilty of murder."

The same fundamental principle is expressed in French law; the *Encyclopédie Dalloz* puts it as follows:

"The defence should be proportionate to the attack, and all excess must be avoided, especially in the legitimate defence of property. Unless there are extenuating circumstances, excessive acts of self-defence are not justified."

And *Donnedieu de Vabres—Droit Criminel* states on page 233 that "the fact that one has been attacked does not mean that it is legitimate in resistance to inflict unlimited harm on the aggressor."

We would, I think, be wise to recognize in the nuclear age that a similar limiting principle is inherent in the right of individual or collective self-defence referred to in Article 51 of the Charter of the United Nations. It is on this Article that the North Atlantic Treaty, the Manila Pact, the Inter-

American Treaty of Reciprocal Assistance, and the other defensive alliances of the free world rest.

Nor is this limitation on the amount of force which can justifiably be used in self-defence considered by civilized society as conditional on a reciprocal and prior recognition of such limitation by an aggressor. The principle is one that civilized men should observe for its own sake, and for the sake of their civilization. If violence breaks out, the play of this principle helps to limit the breakdown to the minimum needed to defeat aggression and, above all, to restore the peace.

If a nation uses force in aggression against its neighbour, that neighbour and its allies, and indeed the entire free community, acting through and within the principles of the United Nations Charter, may justifiably use—in fact have an obligation to use—collective force to repel that aggression. This does not, however, give them a moral licence to attempt, by the use of overwhelming and unlimited force, to destroy completely the aggressor society.

It may be argued that any doctrine which suggests a limitation on the power of the deterrent would merely make aggression more likely and its success easier. The principle in domestic law, however, has had no such effect and, though the circumstances are very different, it need not have such an effect in the society of nations. In any event, without such a principle the very existence of the human race may now be placed in jeopardy by the action of one man or of a few men.

Bearing on this doctrine of force limitation is a cliché which has become popular during recent decades, that "peace is indivisible." In one sense this is undoubtedly true, but it is false in another. Its truth lies in this, that in our interdependent world the insight is sound which proclaims that an outbreak of hostilities anywhere is a proper matter for concern to all nations everywhere, for it is a breach of the peace and the resulting violence may sweep over the earth.

The concept of the indivisibility of peace is, however, false, and even dangerous, if it is taken to imply that a local outbreak of hostilities must necessarily and inevitably lead to global conflict and should be dealt with accordingly. There is always, of course, this risk—a very real risk indeed as I have tried to point out. Yet if it were considered to be a certainty, such a theory could very easily mislead one side or the other to take, or apprehend and seek to forestall, large-scale measures which would indeed make the risk a certainty.

In this connection I believe that the instincts of governments proved sounder than much of orthodox military and political doctrine, when against purely military logic (if there is such a thing) the Korean war was kept localized, when the Indochinese conflict was localized, and when hostilities between the Arabs and the Israelis were localized.

Our spiritual leaders have always proclaimed that all humanity is one family and, in a sense that is more than merely figurative, one body. This fact is becoming increasingly obvious in other than spiritual ways, with the growing material interdependence that technological advances are bringing. If, however, this human family is to survive, we must hasten and deepen our awareness of the implications of its unity, and begin to act accordingly. If we are one body, and a finger is cut, it is neither necessary nor wise to amputate an arm. There is no Biblical injunction counselling a life for an eye!

It is, however, not enough to have a doctrine that restrains us from resorting to any force in certain circumstances, and to unlimited force in others. We need also a doctrine regarding the purposes for which force will be used, if its use ever becomes necessary.

In this connection another cliché, the examination of which is, I think, overdue, is that the object of war is victory. Again, in one sense, this is true, but it is not the whole truth. The slogan can become indeed merely camouflage for mental laziness. To the extent that it is accepted as the whole truth, as it was accepted by many, in the Western democracies as elsewhere, in the two great wars of this century, it is apt to lead to wars of long duration and unparallelled violence; to a military strategy based on total destruction and unconditional surrender, without much thought for the political situation that will follow victory. It leads, in short, to the experience, which we know too well, of winning the war and failing to win the peace. And it is peace, even more than victory, which is the ultimate object of war.

This is the reason why even in the midst of war

we should keep our eyes, not only on military victory, but also on long-term objectives that go beyond the period of hostilities; remembering that though tyrannical regimes and evil ideologies are transient, the races of mankind will live on so long as life itself endures on this planet. It is foolish, therefore, carelessly to introduce, however righteous one's cause, a deep and lasting irreconcilability into the family of peoples.

Men may feel—indeed are bound to feel—bitter and resentful about wrongs and cruelties and sufferings inflicted by the enemy of the moment. Such feelings may be understandable and justified. Despite this, in an age when several governments possess or inevitably soon will possess the capacity to destroy all civilization, it is essential never to forget that now, more than ever before, the fundamental and overriding purpose of sound statesmanship must be conciliation, and the creation of good-will between peoples.

If hostilities ever again break out, surely every effort must be made, not only to prove that aggression does not pay by repelling and defeating the aggression, but also to localize the hostilities, to bring them to an end as soon as the limited objective is accomplished; and then to work at once for a peace which will be just but not savage, the kind of peace that will not have planted in it the seeds of future war.

Until recently, the record of democracies in this century and in this matter has not been such as to give us much reason for satisfaction. In the two world wars, public opinion in the free world has worked itself into violent passion against a ruthless aggressor. The task of repelling an attack has turned into a crusade for righteousness, and into such sweeping purposes as making the world safe for democracy.

While the fighting is raging and the result undecided, detailed consideration of political objectives has often been pushed aside on the grounds that it would divide opinion within a democracy and among allies. In practice this has meant that our peace aims have tended to become confused with a single war aim of destruction and defeat of the enemy, a confusion which has made for post-war difficulties and failures.

It is worth recalling, and benefitting from the experience, that only a few years after the fatuity of the Morgenthau plan for reducing Germany to the level of a subsistence agrarian economy, we are welcoming a rearmed Germany into our coalition. In the passion of 1945, Japan was to be reduced to impotence and in the anxiety of 1955 she is being exhorted to greater armed power. Hostility between the same states is seldom a permanent condition, and war for general or unspecified objectives has rarely made for enduring peace.

There is, of course, one vitally important exception to all this. If an aggressor should launch an all-out thermo-nuclear attack on the centres of our life and civilization, we would be forced to reply in kind and, I am sure, without limitation or restraint. In such an eventuality the aggressor's attack would be far more than an act of war. It would be an act of suicide, and something not much better for his victorious victim. A defence policy of certain and massive retaliation in these circumstances, therefore, is the most effective deterrent, and the best available strategy. There is, I suppose, no present alternative to it, though it is no long-range solution for the problem of peace and war. Yet no-one gets much comfort or any feeling of real security from the thought that peace—or at least the absence of war—rests precariously on a hydrogen bomb, and that, as a stabilizing force, the balance of terror has replaced the balance of power.

The awful catastrophe of total hydrogen bomb attack, then, is one thing. If, however, aggression on any lesser scale breaks out, it seems to me to be vitally important that the force—political and military—used against the aggressor should be for a limited and declared purpose.

Nations were more sensible in this regard in the eighteenth and nineteenth centuries than they have been in this. They fought wars then for limited and specific purposes. The negotiated settlements which ended them (usually before the total surrender of the enemy's forces and often, indeed, with no clearcut military victory for either side), often led to a long period of peace—with, incidentally, some advantages to the side that proved the stronger!

It may seem paradoxical, but military actions to

achieve these purposes which were usually self-interested and materialistic, were not only less bloody but more apt to produce a tolerable result, than our twentieth century popular democratic crusades. In such crusades almost everything becomes total: war, arms, diplomacy, victory, defeat and retribution, and popular emotion. Unfortunately total wisdom and understanding and foresight do not always accompany these other manifestations of totality.

In these earlier times it was possible to compromise about interests, even in war, and thus bring the hostilities to a negotiated close. Today if your war is, or is made to appear as, a great crusade for righteousness and nothing else, even the consideration of compromise is a sin. Furthermore, history shows that men kept greater control over the consequences of their actions when their eyes were on specific and limited political objectives and when their military dispositions were taken with these political purposes in mind.

I doubt whether the *unconditional* surrender of a great nation has ever, in any war, been a very sensible political objective, though it is likely to be a popular political slogan. In any case, it is certainly inappropriate to an international police action, and nowadays is likely to have results which will make the question of ultimate strategic aims academic.

I have suggested that, except in the event of a reciprocal spasm of mutual annihilation, the free world's force should be used only for limited political objectives, of which the chief will be to deter aggression; or if it breaks out, to localize it, defeat it, and prepare the way for a peace settlement.

This is something different from the doctrine of massive retaliation. It is less a matter of punishing the aggressor than of defending the area of freedom and preventing another conflict.

May I give two illustrations?

At the ministerial meeting of the NATO Council held in Paris in December 1954 we took a decision of which one feature, which seemed to me particularly significant, was that it made possible the development of plans for the tactical use of atomic weapons for the defence of the NATO area to supplement the already existing plans for defensive strategic use. At the same time a form of strategy was agreed on, which in the event of aggression against Western Europe should enable SHAPE to defend more effectively the territory of the European NATO members by the provision of a shield which would have a good chance of holding the attack. A feature of great significance in this new strategy, which is based on new strength, is that it should ultimately make it possible for NATO to rely less exclusively on the nuclear capacity to retaliate against the centres of Russian life and to rely more on NATO's ability to hold and throw back the invading armies.

Similarly, the action of free nations against aggression in Korea has been limited, and has had as its purpose not the destruction of the North Korean and Chinese people but the localizing of hostilities, repelling the attack, and then negotiating cease-fire agreements as a prelude to peace. Admittedly these incomplete situations and limited policies create disappointments and frustrations among certain sections of Western opinion. The explanation, may I suggest, lies less in the possibility that the situations themselves have been ill-handled than that these sections of opinion have not thought through—or been fully informed about—the realities of the problem, or the long-run purpose of the action that had to be taken.

Recent experience has driven home another truth: that strategy should be the servant of policy. When it tends to become the master, as it did in the two world wars, victory, not surprisingly, will result in costly and complex new problems that not only hindsight but a profounder and more balanced foresight should have been able to avoid.

Clausewitz's famous dictum that "war is the continuation of policy by other means" has usually and popularly been interpreted, in Clausewitz's homeland and elsewhere, merely as a cynical justification for the use of force. Its central point is, I suggest, more profound, and lies in the recognition that military force should be regarded as an instrument of foreign policy; that sound strategy has never been purely, or even primarily, a military function. I doubt whether, above the tactical and logistic level, there has ever been sound advice or wise decisions which have been exclusively military. Such decisions would result in a confusion of ends and means and the falsification of priorities inherent in the pursuit of inadequate and short-sighted objectives.

If, however, there is to be the proper relationship between military and political considerations in the professional advice given to the elected leaders of democracies, who must in our system make the final decisions, then there are a number of organizational and institutional corollaries. If strategy is to be the handmaiden of foreign policy, it follows that in war strategic advice must be based on a blending of military and political considerations, and that in peace recommendations on foreign policy must embody, appropriately weighed and digested, assessments of military as well as psychological, economic and other political factors.

This means that diplomatic officers, as they approach the levels at which they will have responsibilities for important policy recommendations, should have a full and mature understanding of military factors; and that military officers, as they approach the same levels, will need to have as part of their professional training, an understanding and awareness of political and diplomatic factors.

In recognition of this need we in Canada established shortly after World War II a National Defence College, where selected officers of the Colonel-Brigadier level or equivalent from each of the three armed forces and from the diplomatic and other related civilian services study together, for a year, the sort of long-range problems which do not fall exclusively within the responsibility of any one branch of government. Similarly the United States set up a National War College. The Imperial Defence College in London had already been operating in this field for a generation. In Paris in 1951 a NATO Defence College was established, where a somewhat comparable purpose is sought on an international scale. These are all moves in the right direction at the level of professional training.

There is also the related problem of developing appropriate machinery for formulating strategic directives to task forces or theatre commanders, and for strategic appreciations and drafts of directives on defence programmes. This machinery should be such that at the professional level there is a thorough blending of military, political, and other foreign policy considerations, before matters are referred to governments for decision.

This organizational blending of what I might call military and foreign-policy judgment, was conspicuous by its absence in the leading democracies during the two world wars of this century. The idea seemed to be that once a war began, foreign policy should take a back seat and military policy become, if not an end in itself, subservient only to a generalized military objective such as "total victory" or "unconditional surrender."

It is no criticism of the men concerned, but it is, I think, a legitimate criticism of the system, to suggest that a primarily military approach to the various objectives of war-policy had something to do with the disenchantments of victory. Among the western allies during World War II Chiefs of Staff committees were normally composed exclusively of professional members of the armed forces, as was, on the international plane, the combined Chiefs of Staff. Such harmonizing of political and military control and policy as there was took place "on the summit." This is not always the most comfortable or effective spot for such a process; the winds blow hard and the atmosphere is rarefied!

The relative eclipse during wartime of those who give advice on foreign policy, and their lack of responsibility for participation in *strategic* decisions, rendered almost inevitable a post-war balance of forces which made the organization of peace disappointing and difficult.

Today, there have been significant changes in national organization in many of the leading democracies which reflect, I believe, a sounder awareness of the real problems. There have also been changes in international organization which reflect the same awareness, for these same problems exist within coalitions on a much more complex scale. It would be foolish to imagine that either nationally or internationally the organizational problems are yet all resolved. It would also be foolish to imagine that they could be resolved by trying to push too fast or too far in a direction which, though it might satisfy the requirements of formal logic, would go beyond what is at any given time practicable as determined by the evolution of thought in the various countries and services concerned. But it is only by keeping one's theory ahead of practice that it can serve as a guide to decisions, and only with such a guide can men have much assurance that development will be in the right direction.

CHAPTER III

COALITIONS: THE NEW UNITS

OF POLICY

In introducing this lecture series I suggested that an essential characteristic of the international problems which are apt to appear so overwhelming to our generation is not so much their newness as their gigantic scale. They are, fundamentally, the age-old problems of man's political life, encountered either within his own state or in its relations with other states.

I tried to examine this change in scale with respect to the greatly increased force now available as an instrument of policy, and some of the problems that this has caused or accentuated.

I propose now to survey—though it can only be sketchily—what I might call the type of political society on whose behalf foreign policy decisions are taken and actions launched. Here, too, there has been a tremendous increase in scale.

In this new era on which we have entered, the effective unit of foreign policy and strategy is no longer the nation state, however large, but the coalition of such states brought together and held together for certain purposes. This has given great urgency to the problem of cultivating cooperation and unity within the collective system.

The successful management of a coalition—or, to use the older and not quite so respectable word, an alliance—has always been difficult, even in wartime. It has not always been needed in time of peace. Today, however, in a period of "war and peace," it is both difficult and desperately required.

In international relations, as in other things, the confusion of ends and means can cause trouble. One instance where such confusion is likely to occur and become dangerous is in a free people's attitude toward alliances.

Today, coalitions and collective arrangements are more than mere pieces of international machinery designed and constructed to help us find security; they are expressions, however nebulous, of the cohesion and integrity of all free society. Basically, the totalitarian threat is precisely to this cohesion and integrity. Unity and vitality in that society are not merely required for defending it; they are also the essence of what we must seek to defend.

This, I think, is one reason why many of us feel apprehensive about suggestions, which we hear from time to time, that some further expenditure on measures of continental defence, or some different balance in our strategic plans or in our arsenal of weapons, would allow North America to "go it alone," and to dispense with alliances.

Such a policy of entrenched continentalism would seem to me to be a short-sighted one. Politically, it implies that other free and friendly countries are and can be kept outside our own fate, that our allies are merely means to an end. It implies the self-centred and mistaken doctrine that men in Washington and Ottawa are concerned with the freedom of those in London or Paris, Bonn or Canberra, only for our own national reasons of strategy and security.

Force and strategic factors, of course, should not be minimized or forgotten. Nevertheless it is the unity of our grand alliance of free nations as much as, or even more than, the American arsenal of atomic weapons—vitally important though this is—which remains the strongest foundation for peace today.

It is, I think, unlikely that the Soviet rulers will directly challenge democracy in the field in which we have overwhelming strength—modern weapons—and risk thereby their own existence and that of their empire. There is ample evidence that the cardinal principle of Communist strategy is rather to attack us by exploiting what they call "contradictions," by seeking out the spots where they think we are weak. To this end they almost certainly believe that they have least to risk and most to gain by trying to disunite and disintegrate the coalition and, above all, to isolate the United States from its friends and allies.

It is essential, therefore, in the situation which we face, to maintain maximum unity among those nations who are working together to defend freedom and to maintain peace.

We certainly cannot afford to take this unity for granted. Almost all the members of our coalition are democracies with traditions of freedom and self-rule. Whether this will prove a source of strength or weakness in this troubled age will depend largely on the extent to which our peoples are willing and able to cooperate with each other and also, when it is necessary in the common interest, to subordinate less essential national considerations to the wider requirements of the coalition.

The same principle, in essence, applies to relations between members of a free coalition as between citizens of a free democratic state. Among other things this means that policies with which an important minority not only disagree but consider unjust, and an abuse of the majority's power, can only be enforced, if at all, with difficulty. Persistence in such policies, by those in power, strains the cohesion of the entire society and endangers the democratic process in it. The domestic experience of both our countries proves this. We cannot afford international analogies.

A more basic point is that united action in a coalition of democracies as in a single democracy must rest on debate, conviction, and consent. This question of consent becomes particularly difficult, but particularly necessary, in large and relatively heterogeneous national or international communities. If we examine the former we get an indication of the nature of the problems we will face in the latter.

The United States is made up of a number of regions, and anyone, I think, with experience or understanding of American national politics will understand the significance of this. Similarly in a country like Canada, also vast in extent and containing a number of regions, but which was created out of two distinct peoples, different in language, religion, and culture, we have had to devote particular attention to those political arts which can weld into an acceptable working unity peoples of differing traditions and patterns of thought, and with memories of the past which do not invariably make for close cohesion.

Americans and Canadians have both succeeded in this political task of creating on the national scale a unity greater than that with which we started. It is worth recalling how.

The fundamental principle which has guided statesmanship in Canada, since Confederation, has been that on important issues the nation's leaders should seek and pursue a policy which will commend itself to a majority of those in each main section of the country. This is, of course, only possible to the extent that there is among all of us in Canada a sense of restraint and responsibility, an intellectual flexibility and moral stature sufficient to enable the people of one section to understand another section's point of view when it differs from their own, and to respect it even when they disagree.

Canadian unity has been maintained and consolidated, precisely because a sufficient number of our people, in all sections, have developed these qualities of self-discipline to a degree adequate to the challenges and crises which we have faced. If we can today have a positive policy in foreign affairs and defence—issues on which as recently as fifteen years ago we were deeply divided—it is because of the degree of internal cohesion and unity which have thus been achieved.

The situation in the United States has been similar. You too had a war between sections of your people. Ours, which is known among our French-speaking compatriots as a "conquest," took place in the eighteenth century, before the organization of our national unity; yours took place in mid-nineteenth century, after the establishment of your union, which for a few tragic years it broke. National leaders in both our countries should therefore have a ready understanding, and an almost instinctive grasp, of the requirements for obtaining from varied groups and sections support for, or at least assent to, common measures. Statesmen find it worth making great efforts, and displaying great restraint, in order to devise policies which will if possible obtain popular support in *all* the main regions affected. When this cannot be achieved, it is at the least virtually essential to obtain from all sections an acquiescence that is willing and understanding rather than grudging or forced. In large and diversified democracies particularly, successful leadership is no mere automatic process of counting heads.

Successful politicians in a democracy are inevitably schooled to sense quickly, almost before they appear, the first signs of disunity within their own section or nation. They not only sense it but they try to heal it. They have trained themselves, or should have, to weigh before they speak the probable effect of their words on the people to whom they feel responsible.

For the politician of limited vision, these people may be merely his immediate constituents—the voters of his district, his state. The politician of broader calibre, the politician of national stature, will weigh as well the effect of his remarks—be they a prepared speech in a legislature or an off-the-cuff reply to a persistent newsman—on all the various sections of his country. He will weigh this before, rather than after he speaks; otherwise he will not long be a politician of national stature.

Today, however, politicians of even national stature are no longer enough. Indeed, men with merely nation-wide horizons or loyalties can actually do harm to their own nation by words and attitudes calculated to isolate it from the willing and steady support which in today's world any nation, even the greatest, needs.

The situation, then, which we face today within our free coalition, challenges us by demanding the application, to an area and on a scale far greater than anything hitherto tried, of precisely these arts of democratic government which we have long practised at home with success and in which we should be skilled and experienced. This is not going to be an easy challenge to meet. But meet it we must.

For one thing, a coalition of free—and proud—democracies is a very different thing than the monolithic subjugated land-empire which totalitarians seek. In the democratic world an ally and a satellite are contradictions in terms because of the resentments which domination by mere power will always generate among free men.

This means that if we are to make a coalition work, we must accustom ourselves to living within the requirements and within a framework broader than that of our own state.

These demands impose themselves with varying degrees of urgency on different men, of course; and indeed on different nations, depending on the extent to which each one's actions and words affect others.

They concern the politician and diplomat, the general and admiral. Indeed they concern all citizens, particularly those whose remarks are apt to be picked up by the press and radio, often in a sensational way, and carried in a matter of minutes by newspapers and transmitters in all parts of the world.

I have myself, in common with most public men, been on occasions the object of this kind of sudden far-spread publicity. I once mentioned in an address that I had in years gone by lived in Chicago and worked there with Armour and Co., the great meat-packing corporation. Very shortly afterwards a Communist radio reported me as having given away the secret of my warmongering activities at the United Nations by admitting that I was financially interested in the manufacture of armour and other war materials. The reportorial results of one's public statements are not always so amusing!

This acceptance of the over-riding claims of unity, and of the delays and concessions which are sometimes necessary to cultivate it, comes hardest, of course, to the strongest; for a consciousness of strength naturally and properly encourages self-confidence and may induce a tendency to take for granted the acquiescence of others. Here again our domestic experience can be illuminating.

The essence of democracy is the equation of authority with consent, of power and influence with responsibility. The history of democracy could be described, in fact, as the story of the long and difficult path by which this goal has been approached, the account of our successes and failures over the years in solving the problems posed by these equations. To the extent that the influence and power of any individuals or groups within a nation is greater than their recognition and acceptance of responsibility and of the rights of others—to that extent democracy is merely a word and not yet an achievement. The same principle should apply in the relations between nations who are working together for common and good purposes.

The less strong members of such a group will have a special reason to be conscious of the policies and attitudes of the stronger, and will also normally recognize more acutely the perils of disunity within the greater society of which they form a part.

While this is true, they should also recognize and

try to understand the burdens and difficulties of leadership. It is legitimate to be anxious, but not to be morbid about the power of one's big friends. Criticism from smaller states *can* be wise, constructive, and helpful. It can also be carping and hurtful.

It is also important to be able to discern when the public expression of one's critical views will be advisable and necessary and when it will serve merely to foster disunity and, therefore, weakness inside the group. Backseat political driving in a crisis can be both distracting and dangerous. So can bad driving in front. The dangers of both, of bad driving and of back-seat driving, were well illustrated by a cartoon I once saw whose caption reveals the picture: "How often have I told you children not to bother daddy when he is passing on a turn!"

The less strong states in a coalition have a duty to demonstrate, not a surrender of their identity or free judgment, which would be undesirable and impossible, but a sense of proportion and accommodation, and a recognition that the acceptance of leadership and the possession of power warrant special influence and weight in the counsels of the coalition.

The members of our coalition whose outstanding strength gives them such a position of leadership have on their part a special obligation to cultivate the self-denying virtues of patience, restraint, and tolerance, and a decent regard for the opinions of the others.

The harmonising of these essential ingredients for a successful coalition is not easy. It requires effective machinery and, even more important, a real will to consult and to work out common policies. This should come more easily to political leaders of the democracies because of their domestic experiences. Again the national analogy is apposite.

When national action has to be taken, careful and timely consultation with all concerned is the democratic politician's stock in trade. Anyone experienced in the operations of democratic processes, whether in comimttees or cabinets, caucuses, trade union meetings, or boards of directors, knows, or soon learns, the value of having private consultations with his leading associates, before confronting them in public with the necessity of pronouncing judgment on a new issue.

These processes are equally important in a coalition of states. They are not always followed. But I think that today we are making progress to that end, improving our techniques of cooperation and, more important, increasingly acquiring the habit of exchanging views. We are learning the value of prior discussion, not as a substitute for action, but as an essential for united action.

Needless to say, consultation does not mean merely the opportunity to share in responsibility for implementing a decision already taken. Consultation means the opportunity to participate in the give and take of ideas, the weighing of pros and cons, and the formulation of policy based on the highest common denominator of agreement. It is a method of harmonizing divergent interests, a process which makes it possible so to adjust and adapt measures which any one government may have in mind that they are least likely to disturb, and most likely to consolidate, the unity of the greater international society to which we all belong.

This may seem like a "tall order" between a group of sovereign states, varying so much in power and influence as is the case with the members of our Atlantic coalition. It *is* a "tall order," and its achievement will take time. In crisis or grave emergency— or war—something less may seem to suffice or may temporarily have to suffice. But eventually nothing less than a complete acceptance of the necessity of full consultation—of using as well as having machinery for consultation—will be adequate to consolidate a coalition of free peoples, and to forge out of several democracies a unity deep and strong enough for the international situation of risk and menace with which we may have to live for a long time.

This broader responsibility does not in any sense remove or weaken the direct constitutional responsibility of each democratic government to its own nation. It is something additional. It is less a matter of formal agreement between governments than an attitude which must be developed by men, a quality of outlook that must be achieved by politicians, editors, teachers, and businessmen, by all whose views and actions make up public opinion.

For this purpose of consultation, in addition to the diplomatic missions which each government maintains in the others' capitals, we have now such special institutions, to mention only one, as the North Atlantic Council. The work of this Council through its permanent representatives has been encouraging and valuable, and should be enlarged and developed. The periodic ministerial meetings of NATO, at which the Foreign Ministers, and at times also the Defence and Finance Ministers, of the member countries participate, present a more difficult problem. Too often meetings on this level last only a day or so, with a substantial part of the time taken either by set speeches, or by consideration of a draft communique. The Ministerial participants are often as much the victims of a deadline as any cub reporter, and the requirement of exact precision in the language recording a decision becomes secondary to the necessity of being at the airport in two hours so that an appointment can be kept next day at home, thousands of miles away. As a result—and this has happened more than once in the last few years— misunderstandings have been created which could have been avoided if there had been more time for careful and painstaking discussion between all the participants and for an exact and agreed record of the decisions reached, or thought to have been reached.

Consultation is, however, merely a means to an end. What is the end?

Today, it is nothing less than the preservation of our civilization, and possibly even of our existence. In a crisis this could depend in no small part on the extent to which a deep sense of loyalty, and of belonging to the greater whole, has been built up among the populations and especially among the men who form the governments of certain key areas which are at any given time immediately exposed. We must hope that never again will governments or nations have to make the sort of decision which most of the free governments and men of Europe had to make in 1939 and 1940; between the alternatives of surrender or of standing firm, at whatever immediate threat, on the side of freedom. But though we must hope that such trials will not occur again, we should recognize that our success in avoiding them, or surmounting them if they come, will depend not only on the power and determination of individual nations, but also on the extent to which such imponderables as loyalty to the wider community of free men can be developed among leaders and peoples of the coalition.

A loyalty of this kind, a feeling of belonging, requires the development of something more than a military alliance. Today, in NATO, we have a common military policy for the area of its commitments, collective and coordinated defence arrangements which are becoming stronger and more effective. Nevertheless it is desirable, and may in the long-term prove essential, that this common defence policy become the expression of a coordinated foreign policy, and be backed up by complementary policies in the economic and social fields.

These things cannot be kept in water-tight compartments if a coalition, or if even cooperation, is to be strong and enduring. The present relations between the United States and Canada are an illustration of this. Friendly and neighbourly as these are, it is becoming increasingly difficult and may soon become impossible to accept a situation where our border, to which so many "unguarded" references are made, is to be nonexistent for purposes of defence but very much in evidence for tariff, trade, and other economic purposes. This same unhappy development will also result within coalitions when concentration on arms is allowed to obscure and slow up the progress toward community.

Democracy has never been an easy political system to operate. The demands which it makes on its citizens, and particularly on its statesmen, are great. As it expands to the international arena, these demands grow correspondingly. It is, of course, not certain that democracy can prove equal to the stresses of this broader arena in this troubled age. My own feeling that it can is born of my confidence in the ability of the peoples and the leaders of democratic nations to grow into the new situations and to accept the greater self-discipline which the preservation of freedom in an interdependent world requires.

CHAPTER IV

OPEN DIPLOMACY: NEGOTIATING

IN THE SPOTLIGHT

In the heat of World War I, President Wilson launched the slogan "open covenants openly arrived at." He was at least half right, for the secret treaty committing peoples without their knowledge in matters of policy is evil and to be condemned.

There may, of course, be a legitimate function for secret technical agreements to implement policies which are themselves known and publicly approved. For example, the United States and Canada are co-operating in the development of early-warning radar screens in the northern part of my country, for the defence of this continent. The fact of this coopera-tion, and the general principles on which cost and participation are shared between the two countries, are quite properly matters of public knowledge. Technical arrangements embodying details about the locations, ranges, and other operating factors of the installations are often quite properly not. I mention this qualification not as an exception to the prin-ciple of open covenants, but to point it up.

President Wilson's suggestion, however, that open covenants should all be openly arrived at is another matter, and one which is of very doubtful validity. Sir Harold Nicolson, in his wise little book *The Evolution of Diplomatic Method,* quotes Jules Cambon, a French diplomatist of the early years of this century, as stating categorically, "The day secrecy is abolished, negotiations of any kind will become impossible." This assertion is perhaps too sweeping, but as one who has had something to do with public diplomacy, I certainly recognize its force.

We of the West are inclined to flatter ourselves that excessive preoccupation with what is called "face" is an Oriental characteristic. But to democratic governments, and to individual politicians who have from time to time to win elections, the importance of prestige—which is our word for "face" —is also significant and is treated by us as such; at times excessively. Perhaps some day everyone in democracies may be so mature, so wise, and so tolerant as to see unerringly the full truth behind façades, and to care for that truth alone; but that day is not yet. If it were, neither cosmetic manufacturers nor public relations experts would be so busy!

Meanwhile, if diplomatic representatives are to have the freedom of manoeuvre which is required to bring about agreement, and if "face" is to be kept in its proper place, negotiations *in camera* are often better than those before the camera.

If a nation's delegates to an international conference are given rigid instructions, publicized to the world in advance, this can also be a serious handicap. Few things seem harder to abandon than the bold black headline which at the beginning of the conference has announced your policy to the world; few things harder to face than the wrath of the radio or news pundit who, after having already acclaimed that policy to be superlatively wise and one which he has been advocating all along, then finds that it has been changed.

One of the difficulties about "open" diplomacy is that not only the nature but the very function of negotiation may be confused by whipped-up popular emotion.

The purpose of negotiation is the reconciliation of interests, the exploring of a situation in an effort to find some common ground, some possibility of compromise, the seeking of agreement through mutual adjustments. Such adjustments are not made easier, and may well be made impossible, when the negotiators fear that any concession or compromise will within the hour be printed, pictured, or broadcast back home as a capitulation.

A diplomat of an earlier century, de Callières, gave us some good advice on this score, when he wrote:

"The secret of negotiation is to harmonize the real interests of the parties concerned. . . . Menaces always do harm to negotiation since they often push a party to extremes to which they would not have resorted but for provocation. It is well known that hurt vanity often goads men to courses which a sober estimate of their own interests would lead them to eschew. Success achieved by force or fraud rests on an insecure foundation; conversely, success based on reciprocal advantage gives promise of even further successes to come." [1]

If, however, it is true that the function of negotiation is the reconciliation of opposing interests, it is also a stubborn fact of international life that different nations have interests which do strongly oppose each other. Those who ignore that fact or, at the other extreme, try to explain differences of policy solely in terms of all white on one side and all black on the other, live in a world of unreality. To the extent that such men's myths and bogeys determine policy, disaster is likely to result. That is undoubtedly one of our greatest dangers today. It also obstructs and frustrates that reconciliation which is the main function of negotiation, or what Mr. George Kennan once called "the almost lost art of diplomacy."

In serious negotiation, if you succeed in finding a satisfactory and honourable compromise you have not surrendered, you have succeeded. This can be so even where the other party is a potential enemy, providing you have not betrayed honour or vital interest. Agreement in this sense recognizes that your objective must be to turn enmity into toleration in the hope that it may in time become cooperation.

In negotiation with potential enemies we must

---

[1] Quoted in Harold Nicolson's *The Evolution of Diplomatic Method,* p. 63.

recognize that, quite apart from the danger of deliberate aggression there is always, in a tense and fearful world, the risk of accidental war. Hostilities which no-one wanted could quite conceivably be brought about by miscalculation or a misreading or misapprehension on each side of the other's intentions. Whatever the rights and wrongs of a particular situation, such mistakes under modern conditions could be disastrous for the entire world. For these reasons the greatest importance should be attached to measures which can reduce international tensions, lower temperatures, and remove the barriers, whether they be psychological or physical, to communication.

In my view, nothing could be more dangerous in this divided world than a final and complete failure of man's ability to communicate with man across whatever differences of regime or race or economic conditions, across whatever curtains of fear, or iron, or prejudice may exist. As I see it, one of the most vital of our diplomatic purposes should be to keep open and to develop these channels of communication, so that some day, and may it be soon, when *both* sides are willing, they may be used for the process of negotiation and eventual agreement.

Two hundred and fifty years ago Louis XIV said:

"Open negotiations incline negotiators to consider their own prestige, and to maintain the dignity, the interests and the arguments of their sovereigns with undue obstinacy and to prevent them from

59

giving way to the frequently superior arguments of the occasion."

In the eighteenth century, the sovereigns in question were usually individuals. Today they are hundreds of legislators, millions of newspaper readers, radio listeners, or television viewers. Particularly, our sovereigns are voters and they are the subject of every kind of mass appeal and mass flattery by those who want their votes. In such circumstances the inflexibility which open negotiation encourages is apt to harden into complete rigidity.

If the choice has to be made, it may seem easier—though in the long run the results may be more dangerous—to offend the Far East than the Middle West!

It should, however, hearten the timid diplomat or political negotiator to recall that if in 1955 public opinion limits his freedom of action, the demands of Louis XIV could make him lose freedom of more than action; if failure today to make the necessary adjustments to public pressures threatens the loss of a job or an election, the penalty for failure in earlier days was often a fatal pressure against the neck. This is known as progress!

The most highly publicized part, though not necessarily the most important part, of the diplomatic negotiations of the modern world is that carried on at special *ad hoc* conferences called for a particular political purpose. This technique, though not new, is used much more frequently nowadays than in previous generations, partly because it is increasingly the case that multilateral rather than bilateral negotiations are needed to resolve many of our modern problems. This is, I think, a development of great importance, though it can lead to difficulties and frustrations, as the history of the immediate post-war decade shows.

As an occasion for a meeting of negotiators from a number of different countries, each with different interests and viewpoints, but all with the desire to find some measure of agreement, the special conference can play a valuable and effective role in diplomacy. It is worth noting, however, that successful results of this kind have almost invariably been the product, not so much of a single conference as of a series of conferences, each lasting perhaps only a few days, and each preceded by exchanges of views through diplomatic channels, the series as a whole extending over a period of months or years.

In such cases the conditions for success were a common interest which was greater than competing interests, and a common desire for positive results. Such success almost invariably also required long and careful, and for the most part confidential, preparatory work by ministers and officials.

All this is a very different thing from the highly publicized but inadequately prepared conference, held in an atmosphere of drama and suspicion and nervous tension, with far more preparation for public acceptance of the meeting itself than for any good results to come from it.

Indeed, there are situations—and they are sometimes the most difficult and most important ones—where such highly publicized meetings offer the least promising of all methods of negotiating. An atmosphere of drama is inevitably generated when the spotlights of all the world are focussed on a single "parley at the summit." Such an atmosphere may well be a public relations officer's dream, but a negotiator's doom. Where public expectations and excitement are over-stimulated, deliberation is apt to be confused with dullness and compromise with capitulation.

That is one reason why I feel that we might be well advised to leave more of diplomacy to the diplomats. They are trained for the job and they are usually happy to conduct a negotiation without broadcasting the score after each inning.

If governments fail to reach agreement through official diplomatic channels, they can go on trying or, at worst, fail without fury. But when foreign ministers or, even more, when heads of governments meet, with their inevitable retinue of press, radio, and television companions, with experts, advisers, and advisers to advisers, with clever men to work behind the scenes and even cleverer ones to supply the scenes behind which to work, then things tend to become confused and difficult.

In these circumstances there is always the danger that if agreement cannot be reached at meetings on which so much public hope and expectation have been centred, this will inevitably be interpreted as conclusive evidence that agreement will never be possible. The reaction to this may become, in its turn, unnecessarily despairing and pessimistic. Consequently there is a strong temptation to conceal or deny the fact of disagreement or to concentrate on blaming the other person or persons for it.

This is why such phrases as "a full and frank discussion" at which "all avenues to agreement were explored" and as a result "a clearer understanding was reached" are becoming such invaluable tools for the political negotiator when he has to explain a failure or at least an inadequate success.

It is also why communist governments work out their propaganda tactics at conferences so carefully and so long before the conference opens, and why their exploitation of failure, by attributing it to others, continues long after the conference ends.

CHAPTER V

OPEN DIPLOMACY:

THE UNITED NATIONS

There is today a relatively new kind of diplomacy which is usurping many of the old functions and techniques of the profession, and which is particularly vulnerable to some of the weaknesses which I have mentioned. This is diplomacy by and at public international assemblies. Much the most important of these is, of course, the United Nations. Diplomacy here is peculiarly, at times disconcertingly, open; and to all the propaganda winds that blow. It is also open to misunderstanding, and indeed to misuse.

Those, however, who condemn the United Nations because of its inadequacy in this regard forget two things: first, that serious and confidential negotiations are possible, and are practised, at the United Nations; and second, that our world organization may have a more important role to play even than that of providing machinery and opportunity for such negotiation.

As to the first point, I can confirm from experience that this kind of constructive diplomatic activity does take place in and around the United Nations building in Manhattan, but almost never in any of the large public conference rooms. The facilities provided, and used, for such negotiation are rather the Delegates' Lounge, the offices of the various permanent delegations, and one or other of the small committee rooms borrowed for the purpose when no official meeting is in progress. The paths in the garden by the East River, and the nearby restaurants, have also been the scene of successful negotiation. Anywhere serves, in short, providing it is out of earshot and eyeshot and camera shot of those whose intrusion at this stage of the operation merely makes negotiations more difficult if not indeed impossible.

A second consideration which is often overlooked in condemning the United Nations has to do with its basic role in international relations, which may be described as essentially parliamentary.

This parliamentary role provides a good reason for retaining and using the open-forum diplomatic conference such as the United Nations, alongside the traditional diplomatic mechanism. It brings into the open, by discussion and debate, conflicting and competing international interests, as a prelude to their possible reconciliation by confidential negotiation which if successful will lead to publicized agreement. Also, and this is of equal or even greater importance, it recognizes that in addition to their divergent and competing interests, which must be reconciled by mutual adjustment and compromise, the peoples and governments of the world have also interests in common which must be discovered, brought into public consciousness, openly discussed, and served. For negotiation is only one part of diplomacy, though a vital part.

Understanding of this point should help to remove that misapprehension of the real function of the United Nations which often leads to criticism that, while persuasive, may be unfounded. To make a true assessment of the value of the United Nations, it should be considered primarily not as an alternative to painstaking diplomatic negotiations, but as a symbol of the community of nations and peoples, and an attempt to work out the implications of their interdependence, the recognition of which is its starting point. This world community is as yet a very shadowy and insubstantial thing, but it is a goal toward the realization of which we may work. Like all the best symbols of the greatest truths, the United Nations is not an inanimate thing, a badge or a flag; it is human, and alive, made up of men. It is embryonic, certainly, but it has at least the possibility of progressive development into a real community. Is there any other way than this to reach our one world, except that of total destruction and total subjection? Is there ultimately any other kind of world for the hydrogen age?

Tennyson's "Parliament of Man" is a vision for which many men have worked, and not a few have died, to bring to reality in the United Nations. We may still fail to achieve this vision; but we may not. In any case, we have no right to abandon the dream because it has not *yet* been realized in the United Nations' glass palace on Manhattan.

Apologists for the United Nations occasionally ask critics to reduce their fire, by recalling that the United Nations is still young. If they refer to the youth of the organization itself, I have little sympathy with this plea. It is not a matter of years. The United Nations is as weak—but also as strong—as the recognition in this new era by the majority of men of the demands of world community, and their devotion to that ideal. It is the intellectual and moral maturity of men and nations throughout the earth that matters, not the chronology of an organization in Manhattan.

In addition to this living symbol, the United Nations provides in its Charter a set of principles or code of ethics which member governments have promised to observe. This code is not perfect, but it is good. Like most ethical systems, it is observed only in part and its violations command more attention than its observances.

Furthermore, the Charter establishes certain representative institutions. These have the power to set up other machinery, so that what we have is a living constitution, a social organism with possibilities that if not infinite, are great. There is very little in the political field that men could not do through the Charter, if enough men wished to do it.

These representative organs—The General Assembly, the Security Council, the Trusteeship Council, and ECOSOC—are, as I have suggested, more similar to a parliament, or a constituent assembly, than to a diplomatic negotiating conference. A substantial part of their value, like that of national parliaments, lies precisely in the ability to mobilize and focus opinions, to encourage the formulation, expression, and dramatic confrontation, of major viewpoints. By bringing issues out into the public, and ventilating them, throwing light into dark places, and thereby encouraging more care and responsibility by administrative authorities who understandably hesitate to do things of which they would be ashamed if they were publicly examined in a searching forum; by doing all this, the United Nations tends to improve the working of governments. Its function in this respect is analogous to that of a free and outspoken parliament or congress.

Legislatures in the national domains also perform the function of educating the man in the street about national issues, by dramatizing them in public debate. These debates, in the history of states, have performed inestimable services in extending the awareness of national interests and the feeling of national community. In their way, debates in the General Assembly—or in other agencies of the United Nations—can perform a similar role on a world scale, and have indeed begun to do so.

There is another point. What Sir Harold Nicolson calls "diplomacy by loudspeaker" and "diplomacy by insult" is indeed, as he puts it, "a contradiction in terms" in the context of strict negotiation.

But these phrases are aptly suggestive of lively and vigorous debate in a healthy parliament. The "interminable propaganda speeches addressed not to those with whom the delegate is supposed to be negotiating but to his own public at home" [1] can certainly be exhausting and at times infuriating. But they are something with which I suspect any American Congressman or Senator, or any member of a British or a Canadian Parliament, or any French Député, will be as familiar as are those who have to suffer from them in the committee rooms of the United Nations. It is part of the price of democracy —even, or perhaps especially, of democracy in international embryo.

Within the machinery of any democratic national government there are negotiations aplenty, carried on confidentially before or in conjunction with public debate. Government would be entirely impossible without them. These negotiations by discussion, exploration, and compromise take place in offices, between officials in different sections of a department of government, and at meetings of inter-departmental committees. They take place over the lunch table, between individuals each expert in, or responsible for, some field. They take place within party caucuses. Above all, they take place at meetings of national cabinets.

All these gatherings have one thing in common:

---

[1] Harold Nicolson, *The Evolution of Diplomatic Method*, pp. 90–91, London, Constable & Co.

they are private. The privacy is not sinister, it is merely sensible. But neither this principle nor this process contravenes or makes less necessary the very different role of Parliament or Congress. Indeed it would be either meaningless, or fatal to representative government, if it all did not end in the "hurly-burly" and the "cut and thrust" of legislative talk and turbulence.

There is a parallel to this—though not, of course, an exact one—in the debates of the United Nations.

Most of the decisions that are taken after these debates in United Nations bodies, are either "recommendations"—a sort of exhortation, which can nevertheless carry great weight with the more responsible governments of the world—or they are decisions to set up some machinery, temporary or permanent, in which a certain number of governments participate voluntarily for limited purposes.

Now the governments which wished to create and participate in some such *ad hoc* body could, of course, just as easily do so without going to the trouble of having the body established by a resolution, adopted after debate, in the United Nations. The only immediately apparent point is whether or not to put what we might call a United Nations hat on the whole thing. What are the advantages of doing this? There are some in connection with the service of the United Nations Secretariat, but this is not a major point. Essentially, the explanation lies in an understanding of what I have already called the primary function of the United Nations, that of acting as a living symbol of a world-wide community which it is our interest to deepen and make more real.

A few years ago a real need developed for an international organization made up of the free governments of Western Europe, to plan for the allocation of funds provided to them through the Marshall Plan. This was achieved, as you know, through the development of the Organization for European Economic Cooperation (OEEC). Would it not, however, have been better and just as easy to set up the OEEC as a United Nations body? A United Nations resolution could have been passed, providing for the membership which the OEEC in fact has. The organization would have been fully autonomous, and in it the same governments would have had the same influence as they have now; the same men and women would, no doubt, have been appointed to the Secretariat, to perform the same tasks. The only difference would have been the use of a United Nations label. But for such a purpose this difference would not, I think, have been a small one. If the United Nations had not been by-passed in this undertaking, its prestige would have been higher than it is. When that prestige had to be mobilized in 1951 in terms of contributions of armed forces for the international police action in Korea, the increased power which would have been given in Europe to the U.N. symbol by its association with a major international economic initiative, might have been important.

I mention this example to suggest a technique which all democratic governments sincerely wishing to broaden and deepen support for the United Nations among the peoples of the world might bear in mind.

On United Nations activities and achievements in political and security matters, I do not propose to say much here, centrally important though this field is for the work and future of our organization. I believe, however, that political debates and decisions in United Nations bodies do have a bearing, and at times a very important bearing, on the shape of things to come. They have established new states, protected some old states, stood in the way of aggression and, in one notable case, defeated it when it occurred.

No less important is the influence of debates and decisions in the United Nations on the growth of international activities in the social and economic fields, and above all perhaps, in meeting the problems of poverty, disease, ignorance, and backwardness, or what is in U.N. circles called "underdevelopment."

Some two thousand years ago Aristotle, a singularly shrewd observer of political processes, pointed out that once you establish a democratic form of constitution in any society, you make it inevitable that sooner or later the poor will try to use their voting power as a lever to improve their material lot. This, of course, is exactly what has happened in this century in many democratic national states of the Western world, just as it tended to happen in the city states of Greece in the fourth century B.C.

The same thing, as was to be expected, is beginning to occur in our world society on an international scale, in significant part as a result of the establishment of a loose but nonetheless real framework for discussion and decision among the nations. In the United Nations General Assembly, as in the world which it reflects and represents, the "have nots" are in a clear majority. It is not surprising that they realize this, nor that the existence of a constitutional framework in which this majority speak and have votes has served to stimulate greater awareness, by those more fortunate, of the majority's problems and needs. To see the institutions of the international community working themselves out in this way is ground not for cynicism but for hopefulness.

What about the defects of the United Nations?

One serious constitutional drawback, as I see it, is that providing for a veto on membership. The absence of such states as Germany, Japan, Italy, and many others is a real disadvantage, and one likely to increase as these nations grow in strength. There is also the sensitive and controversial problem of Chinese representation. This is not technically a new-member problem, but one of recognition between competing regimes. Certainly the absence from negotiations and discussions—at the United Nations or elsewhere—of the *de facto* power on the Chinese mainland makes very difficult any effective settlement through the United Nations of disputed matters around China's periphery: Korea, Formosa, Indochina. If and when such problems as these are to be dealt with through the world organization, by conciliation, negotiation, or other peaceful procedures (I am not now dealing with direct diplomatic discussions), then either the Communist Chinese must come to the United Nations or the United Nations must go to them. The Far Eastern Conference at Geneva in 1954, though not itself technically a United Nations conference, was a convincing demonstration of this.

It may be that these difficult membership questions can be resolved by what is now called a "package deal," setting aside for the time being the problem which arises where there are two effective authorities dividing states in certain parts of the world. Partition, and the consequent delay in United Nations membership for the divided states, is one of the unfortunate but temporary results of the cold war. We might as well recognize that the adult objection to a membership "deal" lies not in the fact of the package, or the wrappings, but in the contents. Package deals as such are of course merely another word for compromise, for *quid pro quo,* for the traditional method of making progress in any issue, whether of politics or business, where there are divergent interests.

Apart from the membership question, the veto need not, I think, be a matter of major concern in view of the flexibility of the machinery which the United Nations now provides. The Russians cannot now, through their veto in the Security Council, prevent the United Nations from doing things through the Assembly which the required majority of members wish to do and are physically able to do. Such devices as the Little Assembly and the Uniting for Peace Resolution show that it is not beyond the ingenuity of politicians or constitutional lawyers to make progress despite apparent obstacles. As any student of the constitutional history of Great Britain, the United States, or other democracies knows, this flexibility and ingenuity in constitutional law and practice has made essential contributions to the sound growth of democratic societies.

While the absence of certain countries is regretted by all free men, there are those who also see in the participation of the U.S.S.R. and the "cominform" countries a weakness in the world organization. This point of view is worth considering.

Participation in United Nations debates of representatives of the cominform countries, who use the United Nations as a propaganda forum to try to influence public opinion outside their borders, involves, of course, a drastic lack of reciprocity. The Soviet leaders go to enormous lengths, by controls over the movement of people and news, radio jamming, censorship, and through a monopoly of all media of communication, to prevent debates in the United Nations from having any influence on public opinion in communist countries.

The essence of the Iron Curtain lies in its attempted denial of any community between the people within the communist empire and the outside world. Indeed, this fear of any genuine development of community between individuals or groups of men is fundamental to the nature of Soviet totalitarianism, which abhors spontaneities and freedoms of any sort. The communist rulers therefore attempt to prevent the growth of a living community among their own subjects. What we outsiders see as an Iron Curtain is merely the edge of a horizontal system, a sort of iron blanket, which the men in the Kremlin and in Peking have spread over a third of the earth's territory and over nearly a billion of its people.

This Iron Curtain or blanket strikes at the heart of the United Nations conceived as an approach, however embryonic and imperfect, toward a parliament of man. One of the basic concepts of communist leaders with regard to relations with the rest of the world in every field is that of the one-way street. We would deceive ourselves if we did not recognize this.

Nevertheless, though communist leaders fear to let their subjects see and hear the world as it really is, our own interests lie in the reverse conception. Democracies should fear lest their citizens see less than the whole picture, reflected in full, "warts and all" and so far as possible in the right proportions. Anything short of that is capitulation to the doctrine we are opposing.

This means, so far as membership in the United Nations is concerned, that the Assembly would be less useful to the democracies themselves if communist representatives were not present. The presence of delegations from the communist countries in Europe, and experience with the intransigence of members of the Soviet bloc, have done much to educate opinion, both among the public and among diplomats of scores of countries, on the difficulties and also on the proper methods of dealing with Russians. The communists have exposed themselves, in their strength and their weakness, to our gaze and we should gain by the exposure even if the film is infrared!

Communist participation has also done much to promote cohesion among the non-communist governments of the world. This is not the main reason why I see value to the free world in the participation of communist countries, but it is one reason. I commend it to those impatient people who think that the United Nations would be more useful if the Russians and their associates were outside. Their wish, if granted, might react against them.

The basic reason, however, why I attach importance to the participation in the United Nations of the Soviet Union and its satellites lies in the ideal, however embryonic as yet its realization, of a world-wide international system or community. Recognition of this ideal in some form serves to remind us of our ultimate and underlying kinship even with our opponents. There is a value to this which, if we retain any humility, we will not despise.

Professor Butterfield has put this view clearly and well in a recent book: [2]

"If you possess an international order or it is your desire to assert the existence or the authority of

---

[2] H. Butterfield, *Christianity, Diplomacy and War,* pp. 96–97, London, Epworth Press.

such an order, you are the party which must refrain from conceiving the ends of war [even, I might add, a cold war] as though you were fighting barbarous hordes entirely outside the system. . . . So long as an international order exists, or so long as we might desire one to exist, wars must come short of the last degree of irreconcilability and must retain some of the characteristics of a conflict between potential allies, some trace of the fact that they are quarrels between friends."

The supreme goal of our policy must be to make secure the kind of peace which will be consistent with the integrity of our free society. In this search, coalitions for collective security have a vital part to play. Naturally these coalitions, such as NATO, which are designed to deter aggression, do not include in their membership those nations whose actions have inspired the fear and mistrust which brought about the establishment of the defensive coalition. But the United Nations has a deeper and longer-range purpose to serve even than deterrence, that of reminding us that our ultimate goal must be conciliation, and the development of a community in which all our fellow men will one day participate with us. It is important therefore that even potential aggressors remain inside the universal organization for reconciliation and cooperation.

This is why I have emphasized the value of such representative bodies as the assemblies and councils of the United Nations: not because, in themselves, they are the only or necessarily the most effective forums for negotiations, but because the obligations they impose on governments to take a public stand on various matters does in fact induce negotiation; and because they can keep always before our eyes the aspirations and objectives of world policy directed in the common interest of mankind.

To sum up, an essential role of the United Nations, as I see it, is to bring the major world problems into a true focus by showing them in their just proportions and against the background of our underlying community of interest. I ventured to put this point of view in my remarks in the opening debate of the 1954 session of the U.N. General Assembly. I said then:

"The evolution of technological processes and developments in nuclear science have made mankind far more immediately interdependent than either public opinion or governments, in any part of the world, have yet realized. But, unfortunately, as our interdependence increases, our divisions persist. The undeniable fact that if we do not find a means to harmonize, to reconcile them, they may destroy us all, increases the importance of the United Nations as a centre of negotiation, of reconciliation, and of unity. By unity, however, I do not mean the lifeless uniformity which is the ideal of totalitarianism.

"If we are to do anything about these divisions, we must first recognize and try to understand them.

"There is, first, the fundamental division between totalitarian and free societies. In the former, the citizen is the mere servant of the state, while, in international matters, reliance on force and aggressive expansion is a normal development, however much the words "peace" and "co-existence" may be used to camouflage or confuse. Free societies, on the other hand, are based on the doctrine, however imperfectly realized in practice, that man has rights and duties above and beyond the states and governments which have been created by him in order to protect his freedom and security under law and justice.

"Then there is the division between the self-governing and non-self-governing parts of the world. Many people often, but I think mistakenly, equate this division with that between colonial administering countries on the one hand, and the dependent territories on the other. In fact, of course, the non-self-governing part of the world is incomparably greater than this. A people who are governed by a dictator, whose power is based merely on military or police control, is not self-governing, even if the dictator happens to be of the same race, and to speak the same language as most of his subjects. The people of a puppet state, the satellite dictatorship of a totalitarian power, are non-self-governing to a greater extent than the people, for example, of a colony which is on the move, though sometimes the move may seem to be too slow, to national freedom under democratic self-government.

"Then there is the distinction between the highly industrialized parts of the world, with relatively advanced material standards of living, and what are called the "underdeveloped" areas. Under the leadership of the United Nations we are trying to do something about this, but the process we are finding is bound to be a slow one. I hope it remains steady.

"The United Nations, then, operating in a world thus deeply divided, and indeed made the more necessary precisely because of that division, represents and must try to serve men on each side of each of these divisions, without betraying or weakening the principles of its Charter in the process.

"Our direction is clearly laid down: it is toward economic and social progress and away from poverty: it is toward full and free self-government and away from dictatorial regimes imposed from inside or from outside: toward the progressive realization of human rights and the dignity and worth of the individual person."

CHAPTER VI

RELATIONS BETWEEN CIVILIZATIONS

Thus far, in our examination of some implications of the new scale on which problems of democracy and world politics now present themselves, we have reflected on the terrifyingly increased force now available to men as an instrument of policy, and on the enlarged international communities on whose behalf policy decisions have to be taken. This was followed by a review of the nature and function of international organizations, particularly the United Nations, and of the practice of diplomacy and the conduct of negotiation under the conditions of today.

There is another respect in which foreign policy problems present themselves to our generation in a new order of magnitude: this concerns the relations between civilizations.

The major issues of diplomacy for several centuries have, for the West, been reflections of the changing relations between the various states of Europe. Today the most far-reaching problems arise no longer between nations within a single civilization but between civilizations themselves.

When one looks at Asia today, the fact that stands out above all others is the renaissance of its ancient life and cultures. Throughout the East there is a vigorous upsurge, a new vitality. A century ago the

Orient gave the impression of stagnation, with its great periods of achievement behind it, with only a brooding nostalgia over a splendid but abandoned past. Today the peoples of the Orient are eager and restless with visions and strong in their determination to achieve new goals of freedom and welfare.

This is something which all men of good-will should welcome. The yearning and the effort of the people of the Islamic world, of India, and of Southeast Asia to move towards a new and fuller life, somehow to combine modern technical achievements with the spirit of their own cultures and traditions, is exciting and can be full of promise for the world.

The vitality and depth of this resurgence should neither be underestimated nor misinterpreted. It would be absurd to imagine that these new political societies coming to birth in the East will be replicas of those with which we in the West are familiar. The revival of these ancient civilizations will take new forms. It will be different and full of interest to those with the humility and awareness to learn.

In the past all great civilizations have in their periods of growth tended to be expansive—"imperialistic," if you will. This has been true both in the East and in the West. Hitherto the normal relation between such expanding civilizations has been conflict and war, or at best an uneasy truce. We are now emerging into an age when different civilizations will have to learn to live side by side in peaceful interchange, learning from each other, studying each others' history and ideals and art and culture, mutually enriching each others' lives. The alternative, in this overcrowded little world, is misunderstanding, tension, clash, and catastrophe.

This pattern of reviving Asian civilizations is now marred by the threat of totalitarianism. Every progressive move in the past has to some extent been menaced by a barbarism that surrounds and underlies it. But today for the first time we find that all of man's civilizations are collectively threatened, and that some are for the time being largely submerged, by a new form of barbarism which is massive, organized, and ruthless.

In an age which has had experience with Italian Fascists, German Nazis, and Russian and Chinese Communists, it should not be necessary to labour the danger from this development of totalitarianism. The virulent denial of values and the pursuit of power as an end in itself can have a terrible attraction for certain types of otherwise intelligent men. The cynical effort to manipulate all things, and all men, as means to the single end of power, can prove to be even a sort of integrating factor, and can generate for a time a strong social dynamic.

Moreover this nihilist dynamic, coated with suitable ideological trappings, has in the less developed countries been able to capture genuine mass movements of nationalism and social progress, and to harness the energies of thousands of sincere and devoted men and women. Within a few decades a handful of communists in Europe and Asia have been able to organize developments in such a way as to bring a form of political and social articulation and effective administration to several hundreds of millions of people.

This has been an amazing and terrible achievement, and its results—in terms of world-wide struggle —have coloured most of our political thinking, created a focus for most of our fears, and prompted much of our diplomatic activity since 1945.

But the tendency to see our main international problem as essentially one of dealing with communism, and to view the world solely in the bi-polar terms of cold war, is, it seems to me, dangerously oversimplified. Our essential problems are still with people, and with their civilizations or lack of them. Even in dealing with those who threaten us, effective policy will depend in part on discerning and dealing with the realities of Russian and Chinese societies beneath the Marxist superstructure. Moreover it would, I think, be more realistic and produce better results if in dealing with the dangers to peace in Asia, we talked more about Chinese imperialism, which Asians understand from experience, and less about communism which, as yet and as such, has little terror or indeed even little meaning for the great majority of free Asians.

A study of the lives and times of Russian czars and Chinese emperors is, I think, as valuable for the understanding of our difficulties with Moscow and Peking as an expert knowledge of dialectical materialism.

I do not mean, of course, to minimize the ideological aspect. I believe it is of fundamental importance. But as I shall try to show later, success on this plane lies less in countering communism than in rediscovering the universal values of our own faith. To the extent that we embody these in our policies and actions, it is *our* moral and intellectual force which will prove contagious, and the thin doctrines of communism will be recognized for the reactionary superficialities which they are and have always been.

Essentially, it seems to me, totalitarianism points up and exacerbates a number of the problems which we face. But it did not create most of these problems, and our legitimate preoccupations with it and our fears about it should not be allowed unduly to distract our attention from them.

There have been similar storms in history before now, though none—even that of the French revolution—has had the same sweeping, world-embracing consequences or produced so many anxious and at times feverish reactions as the totalitarian menaces of the twentieth century.

Faced with a common danger from the communist imperialisms of Russia and China, one obvious and necessary response is not merely the drawing together of Western democratic nation states, but also cooperation between whole civilizations which are menaced.

The difficulties in the way of such cooperation, between peoples of fundamentally different ways of life, have a special and deep-set character. The rivalries and fears of European states during the past three hundred years have certainly been bitter enough; and the divergence of interest has been complicated—it still is—by differences of outlook and consequent misunderstanding. It is not easy to replace these rivalries by confidence and cooperation. But despite widely clashing national traditions there has been a basic similarity in education, in thought, and in values, which has facilitated understanding, softened animosities, and made compromise and agreement less difficult.

The obstacles in the way of understanding and agreement between peoples of different civilizations are inherently greater. They are, moreover, increased by the wide differences in material standards of living and, above all, by resentments arising from memories of conquest, colonialism, and racial arrogance. If, therefore, to the problem of reconciling divergent interests—and this in all truth will be hard enough—there is not to be added the complication of deep and basically moral misunderstandings, exceptional effort will have to be made on all sides to develop and to exercise imagination, tolerance, and patience.

The greatest danger of misunderstanding between men of different civilizations lies in the misapprehension of motives. And the first need, if we wish our motives to be clear to others, is that we be clear about them ourselves.

Consider, for example, the matter of economic assistance. The United States, with unparalleled generosity, along with my own country and other main centres of the Western world, are contributing out of their own resources either directly or through international arrangements such as the Colombo Plan, the United Nations, and the International Bank, to the economic and technical advance of economically less fortunate nations.

There are three valid reasons why we do this. One is humanitarian, a sincere desire on the part of those who are materially more favoured to help those who are less. The second is the recognition that it is in our own interest to live in a world where prosperity is more universal; that the more quickly other people's standard of living can rise, the better off all of us will be; that a residential area surrounded by slums is not only disquieting but ultimately intolerable. The third is the hope that economic aid can serve the cause of peace. We believe that the stronger any free nation is, the less likely it is to be attacked, and the less likely, therefore, war becomes.

It is important, however, to guard against any false idea that we can purchase or should try to purchase allies. Communist propaganda is insinuating this interpretation throughout Asia, and it is important to give it the lie. The East will not become a mercenary in our ranks. It would be deplorable if Asians believed that Westerners had insulted their dignity, or misread their integrity, by entertaining such notions.

We must also avoid the superficial idea that the appeal of communism is merely to the hungry, and that a higher material standard of living will remove the appeal. Men are not so simple as that.

This point is worth considering carefully, for it is widely misunderstood. Totalitarians view public opinion essentially as something to be manipulated, or feared, and it is not surprising that they have devoted enormous energy, resources, and thought, to developing methods and instruments of propaganda. Their main techniques are of course by now well known in Western countries—the big lie, systematised and tireless repetitions, and particularly the exploitation of what psychologists call the non-rational association of ideas. This latter technique is, of course, fairly common in some Western business advertising, where it may be innocuous enough. For example, a picture of a pretty girl in a bathing suit is used to advertise a soft drink, or a cigarette, or a motor car. Of course it doesn't follow that if you buy the drink or the cigarette you get the girl. But the advertising does not repudiate this attractive possibility and it often does increase sales.

Similarly, communist propagandists try to associate in people's minds the idea of supporting Russian policies or supporting people who obey Russian orders with the quite different idea of higher wages or more low-cost housing, or with some protest against a real or imagined social injustice. Sometimes it happens that they put their finger on a real social injustice. Sometimes it happens that some of the things they protest against *are* deplorable, and even that some of the things they advocate may be in themselves desirable. But the relation of these causes to communism, or to Soviet (or Chinese Communist) policies, is at best a *non sequitur,* and more often an inversion. Yet this exploitation of the common human tendency to associate ideas that are seen or heard together, whatever their logical connection or lack of it, often does work.

For example, this technique of association did suffice for years to persuade a certain number of people in the Western world that communism was a progressive movement, whereas it is really of course as reactionary as tyranny and as old as sin. It has more recently sufficed to capture a number of nationalist movements and to persuade millions of Asians that communism is opposed to imperialism, whereas the truth, of course, is that communism is now by far the most virulent imperialism of the century.

It is for that reason that I have always been skeptical of facile suggestions that where you have a higher standard of living, or better material conditions, you are safe against communism. It is, as I say, not so simple as that.

It has been found, for example, in France and Italy, that it is frequently the districts with the highest average money incomes that produce the largest percentage of communist votes. Can anyone seriously think that Asians' resistance to communist propaganda will depend on the timely attainment of per capita material incomes at, say, the North Italian level? Intellectual and moral perception does not vary so much with one's standard of living.

I am not, of course, suggesting that the West should not provide economic aid to Asia, nor am I minimizing its importance. On the contrary, I see in such programmes one of the most promising long-range developments in the whole field of world politics.

What I do suggest is that if we of the West provide material aid only or primarily for cold-war motives, we are likely to fail in achieving any good and permanent result. If, however, we do so out of a recognition of kinship with our Asian and other neighbours, then we shall succeed in improving the political atmosphere as well as in promoting human welfare. Good-will is contagious.

While such economic aid is important, it is significant, and worth reflecting on, that it is a basic plank of communist propaganda throughout Asia—and one to which thousands of Asians have given credence—that the West has nothing to offer but technology; no philosophy, merely plumbing; Coca-Cola for Confucius!

By this propaganda the attempt is made to use as evidence against us the very programmes of our co-operation. Meanwhile though the Soviet Union is, for a price, giving aid, both economic and military, to the Chinese People's Republic, their communist followers inside the free Asian countries concentrate on the provision and spread of ideas, of organizing techniques, and of literature. In many of the university and cultural centres of Southeast Asia, a very large percentage of the "serious" books in the humanities and other fields which are available in Asian and European languages at prices which Asian students can afford are the product of communist publishing houses.

It is paradoxical that in relations between civilizations it is not the democracies of the West but the Communists, professed materialists, who, concealing their reactionary and enslaving goals, exploit the truth that man does not live by bread alone, nor defend himself solely by arms.

This emphasis of ours on the primacy of the technical, in the relations between Asians and the West, is a great change from the situation a generation ago. One thinks of the role of Western missions during the past hundred years in furthering understanding between the races of men, of the contribution they have made to the reawakening of dormant peoples, of their achievements in developing schools and hospitals. In the secular field, too, the emphasis until recently was not merely or primarily on the technical. During the first half of this century thousands of young men from India studied law, history, and philosophy in the universities of Britain. In significant part the recent history of the Indian subcontinent is the story of their post-graduate activities.

Today, also, thousands of students from Asia and Africa are studying in the United States, Canada,

Britain, and other Western countries on fellowships provided by such schemes as Point Four, the Colombo Plan, and United Nations programmes. It is significant however that these fellowships are now taken up very largely by students in engineering, science, and other technical fields. This training is, of course, important and admirable, so far as it goes. But does the balance of subjects in these exchange programmes really reflect the West's judgment as to the relative importance, for national development and international relations, of the various branches of education? Personally I would like to see a Learned Hand on a mission to Asia as well as the most learned engineering brain.

Much might be accomplished, for example, if provision were made for the exchange of university lecturers and students in history or politics or philosophy, and for visits of editors and newspapermen. In addition to sending Western machines, it would be important to make readily and cheaply available to students in Asia some of the works of the leading thinkers whose insights have shaped Western civilization and, similarly, to make provision for Asian assistance in broadening the facilities, in our own centres of learning, to study these older civilizations.

More contacts between Asia and the West in the cultural fields and the humanities could, I think, prove of great importance. It is the philosophers, teachers, and writers who in the long-run largely shape the public opinion of any people. In these fields, certainly, relations between the West and the renascent culture of Asia would be no one-way street; here we could get as well as give.

In this connection I was impressed by something my friend Charles Malik, the Lebanese Ambassador to the United States, said to the World Council of Churches when it met in Evanston in the summer of 1954:

"For all their intricacy, the political, social and economic problems of Asia and Africa are nothing compared to the intellectual and spiritual problems. For we can already see with some assurance that if people do not yet completely rule themselves, they will sooner or later; if people are not yet fully able to exploit their own resources, they are on the way to doing so; and if social discrimination and injustice still prevail, the one pronounced temper of the age is precisely to attack them. In these fields we can see ahead, albeit more or less dimly.

"But what is going to happen to the mind and soul of Asia and Africa?—that is the question. Nor is it true that once people have achieved their political independence, once they have attained economic plenty, and once they have brought about social justice, the spirit then will take care of itself. This is the greatest fallacy of the present age, that the mind, the spirit, the soul of man, the fundamental bent of his will, is derivative from, subordinate to, a function of, his economic and social existence."

Before leaving this subject of understanding between systems of society and civilizations, I would like to mention—and it can be only to mention—the unique role which may be played in this matter by the Commonwealth of Nations of which Canada is privileged to be a member. This is a loose but intimate association which includes in its membership nations from each of the continents. Its value as a bridge of understanding between the West and Asia and Africa is very great in this age of suspicion and strain where there are few such bridges.

Incidentally it is, I think, worth reflecting that the value and strength of the Commonwealth association in international relations flows largely from the fact that it is based essentially on imponderables. If the Commonwealth had developed in a direction of integrated constitutional machinery, it could not conceivably have possessed the flexibility and capacity for growth which has made possible the willing membership in it of Asian nations as well as of peoples of European origin. The strength of the Commonwealth lies precisely in the undefined but genuine recognition by its members of the value to each of such an association with the others, and of a common interest in the preservation of a system which includes us all. Such recognition would be a good basis also for a wider international order.

CHAPTER VII

DEMOCRACY AND THE POWER

OF DECISION

Thus far, in our consideration of the new scale on which the problems of world politics present themselves to our generation, we have for the most part looked outward from ourselves—at force as an external instrument, at societies and associations greater than the national, and finally at the relations between civilizations.

This enlargement of the scope and scale of our international problems has been accompanied by—some say hopelessly complicated by—the increase within democratic states of the number of people who take part in determining the essential decisions of foreign policy. The vast majority of them do this indirectly, though decisively, through their votes. A growing number intervene more directly through the agencies that influence opinion, agencies such as press, radio, or television which can remove—or create—prejudice and ignorance. Increasing also, in certain forms of democratic rule, is the intervention of the individual member or committee of the legislature in the day-to-day decisions on and administration of foreign policy, something which has been traditionally the main responsibility of the executive.

I have already mentioned this development in connection with the techniques of diplomacy and negotiation. I would like to say a word about it now in regard to the formulation of policy.

Popular participation in foreign policy decisions in some form is, of course, inherent in the nature of the democratic process. This is as it should be. Nowadays, in free and democratic countries, foreign policy must not only seek to protect and advance the interests of all the citizens, but its principles and its major moves must carry their understanding and consent as well. Until comparatively recently, even in Western societies, decisions in this field were usually taken by a single ruler, or a few members of a ruling class. Sometimes, indeed, policies sought only to serve the interests of those few. Today it is very different. We are all concerned now. We are all masters and all servants. We are also all experts!

Those who today fear the confusing intellectual and emotional effect of legislative and popular intervention in the execution of foreign policy, who complain about the alleged prejudices and the unwise purposes that inspire much of this intervention, should not forget that selfish and unprincipled influences could also be and often were exerted in former years in the highly centralized government of a monarchy or a small group. The palace favourite, the courtier, or even the clown could, I suspect, often operate to obstruct good and wise decisions, or alter and confuse a carefully thought out foreign policy in the same way that mass opinion and mass appeal can today. Countermeasures in those earlier days by the monarch's wise and patient foreign minister against a palace clique may, however, have been easier and more effective—though entailing no doubt greater personal physical risk—than those which a Secretary of State or a Foreign Minister can take today against a newspaper columnist, a radio commentator, or a legislative subcommittee!

Democracy may make for more numerous and more varied interventions in the control and execution of foreign policy. Autocracy certainly makes for more deep-set and sinister intrigue—as Moscow is our witness. A Secretary of State may lose some prestige and power if a legislative committee thinks he is a "deviationist" from what they feel to be wise and patriotic policy. A Foreign Commissar will lose far more than prestige if he finds himself in the same dilemma and running counter to the views of one or two or three dictators.

The fact remains, however, even though some of the worries caused by it may be unfounded, that the views and attitudes of millions of people, informed, misinformed, and uninformed, now play an important part in the formulation of policies.

It is often argued that the mass of people, in whom rests this final power, find it peculiarly difficult to face up fully to their responsibilities and to take the hard decisions, the wise rather than the opportunist ones, which may be required. Certainly history affords many instances of democratic inadequacy in this regard.

Twenty-three hundred years ago, in the pure, if restricted, democracy of Greece, there was a face-to-face relationship between people and leaders, the kind that television is reintroducing, at times with somewhat dubious results. Direct contact of this kind didn't always make for conviction, however, in those days, any more than it does today. You will recall how Demosthenes tried in vain to rouse the Athenian Assembly to the threat from Philip of Macedon, and how he failed, just as Sir Winston Churchill failed in the 1930's to rouse the British Parliament to the threat of the Nazis.

Thucydides tells us how, in 427 B.C., Cleon told the Assembly, "I have often before now realized that a democracy is incapable of empire . . . ." The reason for this incapacity, Cleon suggested, is that the members of the Assembly forget that other people are not like themselves. "The most alarming feature in the case," he asserted, "is the constant change of policies, and seeming ignorance of the fact that bad laws which are never changed are better for a city than good ones that have no authority." Cleon went on to describe his public—and to their face—in these terms:

"The persons to blame are you, who are so foolish as to institute these debates: you go to see an oration as you would to see a sight, you take your

facts on hearsay and judge of the practicability of
a project by the wit of its advocates, and trust for
the truth about past events not to your eyes but
to your ears—to some clever critic's words."

It has a contemporary ring, except that politicians
today do not often talk like that to their electors.

Twenty-six centuries or so later Mr. Walter Lippmann, analyzing as "a field of equations" the series
of interdependent choices with which government
policy makers are faced, concluded that

"faced with these choices between the hard and
the soft, the normal propensity of democratic governments is to please the largest number of voters.
The pressure of the electorate is normally for the
soft side of the equations." [1]

From this Mr. Lippmann draws the depressing
conclusion that it is safer for a democratic politician
to be wrong before it has become popular to be
right, and tempting for him to keep in step with
opinion rather than with events.

Mr. Lippmann is inclined to blame this on the
pressure of mass opinion on government, on the con-
tradictory character of mass purpose in using this
pressure to attain policy objectives. To him "public
opinion becomes less realistic as the mass to whom

---

[1] Walter Lippmann, *The Public Philosophy*, pp. 45–46, Atlantic,
Little Brown, 1955.

information must be conveyed and argument addressed grows larger and more heterogeneous." [2] This, he feels, accounts in large part for the conflicting and confusing nature of the pressures developed. These also tend to grow more and more passionate and insistent and dominating; and, according to Mr. Lippmann, "where mass opinion dominates, there is a morbid derangement of the true function of power."

It is not necessary to agree with the whole of Mr. Lippmann's thesis on this matter to admit that he has put his finger on a danger that certainly *can* result from this increase in direct popular determination and control of policy. Such control, if not exercised with responsibility and restraint, can undoubtedly facilitate that type of moral and intellectual deterioration which, throughout history, has preceded and been the effective cause of the overthrow, from within or without, of great societies.

It will help us to understand this danger if we look at one or two aspects of international politics during the last fifty years. One way of learning is trial and error, and we have had a heap of both. But experience in itself, though a valuable channel to wisdom, is no guarantee of it. It should moreover be measured less in how much happens around one than in the quality and intensity of awareness. You may remember Napoleon's comment when someone recommended one of his officers to him for promotion on the ground that he had been through an exceptional

---

[2] Walter Lippman, *The Public Philosophy*, p. 39.

number of campaigns. "My horse," Napoleon is reported to have replied, "has been through even more." As Frederick the Great asked searchingly of his generals: "What good is your experience, if you have not reflected on it?"

If we are to reflect on and benefit from our experience, the first step must be to recall it. May I do so in relation to one matter.

Thirty years ago the thinking of many people in the United States was isolationist. A great number, perhaps the majority of Americans, felt remote from what was going on in Europe and were far from unhappy about that remoteness. They were, if not indifferent, apparently unaware that their own fate might be involved in these far-away matters.

Canadians, because of their history and traditions, though not immune from isolationism, have never felt to the same extent this remoteness from Europe. Canada's entry into war in 1914 and in 1939 was a result (and also, of course, a cause) of this attitude. Nevertheless there were many Canadians in the thirties, as there were more Americans, who hoped that they could sail by the European sirens, their ears stopped with the tax bills and their eyes blinded by the tears of the last great war.

In the twenties and thirties Canadian Governments, however, had another motive, no less compelling, for avoiding European entanglements. This lay in the profound differences of opinion held by various sections of the Canadian people, about the rights and wrongs of European issues and their concern for us. There were, of course, some Canadians, as there were many Americans, who shared the comfortable illusion that the oceans would suffice to protect us, and that our country could remain secure and untouched, outside any European conflict. But Canadian Governments in the 1930's sought to avoid acceptance of political and security responsibilities in Europe or in the old League of Nations, less because they really thought that they could thereby avoid future military commitments if war came, than because they knew that any expression of opinion more precise than pious generalities would involve them immediately in domestic political difficulties at home.

If, in the decade before the Second World War, North America was ineffective in world politics, either through a false sense of security or through the weakness which profound divergences of opinion are apt to bring, the performance of the democracies of Europe was no more creditable and possibly even less so. They were closer to the danger, yet they refused to see it. In many countries this refusal was reinforced by a sort of paralysis of the will which was almost as disastrous as wrong headedness and wrong policies. Intellectual error and inadequacy played their part, of course; but a sort of moral blindness was, I think, primarily responsible for the rot. It was not so much that people did not know that a willingness to accept risks is sometimes necessary to the victories of peace as well as of war, but that, necessary or not, they were unwilling to assume the responsibilities and sacrifices that action would involve.

In the 1930's the Western democracies reached a nadir which had little or nothing to do with political institutions at home or diplomatic method abroad, relatively little to do even with the state of knowledge or intellect, a nadir which indicated something more like moral bankruptcy of societies and of the men who compose them.

In foreign relations and in domestic affairs, too, the 1930's reached a low point. Technically, great progress was made, but a society can be advanced in a technical field and backward in others. The depression was certainly no mere technical matter, with its insulting paradox of idle and hungry men in the midst of abundant resources; and it illustrated, I suggest, a failure of moral insight and social purpose in our society. It seemed almost to be forgotten that men are the most important of any nation's resources, and their welfare the purpose of the economic process.

Then came a cruel and brutal but liberating experience. The development at the end of the thirties of an over-riding and coherent social purpose (even though that purpose had to arise from a war which the democracies a few years earlier might have prevented) drove home to governments and people the lesson that for societies any objective which is both physically possible and passionately desired is financially and politically possible also.

If I recall these ills of democratic society in the

1930's, which one might sum up as *malaise* in foreign policy and depression at home, it is to illustrate the point that no amount of democracy is a guarantee, in internal or external politics, either of good judgment as to methods or of a sound sense of direction as to ends.

It will also remind us of the speed with which a rot can spread when too many people in democratic societies forget their own standards.

Recall of the 1930's serves, finally, to counter present discouragements by reminding us that we have made great progress since then (though not without the appalling cost of war) on the return to political vitality and health.

The malady which Mr. Lippmann warns us against, of indecisiveness, reluctance to face reality or take the necessary but hard decisions, is not, as I see it, inherent in democracy as a political or constitutional system. It is, rather, the result of an internal derangement within individual men. This malady, which is contagious, can hit *any* society if enough men in positions of political influence abdicate their own responsibilities in favour of their special or selfish or superficial interests.

For this purpose, the key difference between a representative democracy and other forms of political society is that in the former every citizen as an elector is in a position to influence a decision; the attitudes of more people have an immediate and significant bearing on political events. When the moral tone of the majority is sound this is a source of strength, a reserve on which the society can draw and which will tend to remove the second-rate or shoddy from elected positions of power. In autocratic or oligarchic societies, on the other hand, the moral and intellectual flabbiness of only a few men in the seats of power will lead to the disintegration of great empires, as it did in 1917 in Czarist Russia.

Democracies are not, then, as I see it, more susceptible than other societies to the political disease which destroys civilizations, and which I have described as a loss of character and a weakening of moral fibre.

The demagogue, for instance, is merely the democratic version of the sycophantic courtier of absolute monarchy. He can reach more people but not, I suggest, bring as much decisive influence to bear on policy. His roars into the microphone are not as effective in this regard as the whisper in the monarch's or the despot's ear.

Just as absolute rulers, however, could be a prey to hypocrisy and insincerity in courtiers, who told the king not what they believed but what they thought the ruler wished to hear, so democracies can never be wholly immune against the same unamiable characteristics in those who seek position or power.

The disease, of course, occurs not only in demagogic politicians. It can develop in a foreign service, or a civil service, or in any other organization of government or of business, if officers shape their reports and recommendations not on their own honest judgment of a situation but on their estimate of whether a particular recommendation is likely to be popular and to earn them advancement now, or be unpopular ten years later, and earn them dismissal then.

This is an occupational hazard which the man of honesty and strength and moral courage will take in his stride.

Similarly, there is nothing in the theory or practice of democratic government which requires a public servant to speak or vote or act contrary to his own judgment of the nation's best interests. Politics has been well called "the art of the possible," and it is not only reasonable but useful and indeed indispensable that the practising politician should, before reaching a decision, make an estimate of the public acceptability of any given course; usually he will be right to adapt his timing and method of presentation to it. But that is a very different thing from acting against his own best judgment of what, all factors considered, the national interest requires. To do this latter is a form of betrayal.

The essential political principle of democracy is what is called responsible government: the provision that the government, if its exercise of power is not approved, can be removed from office by the electorate. This provision is in no sense based on the assumption, demonstrably false in the light of even short periods of history, that the opinion of the majority on every issue is invariably right; but rather on the sound theory that the most appropriate, though possibly not the most expert, judge of good cooking is not the man in the kitchen but the man in the dining room.

So far as I am aware, no democratic constitution beyond the town-meeting level has ever provided that the government should follow majority opinion on each issue that arises. What they do provide, on the contrary, is that the government is accountable either to a legislature or, at intervals of a few years, directly to an electorate. While the persistent flaunting of the conviction of the majority would render government impossible, there is no constitutional or political necessity for governments to be at the mercy of transient tempers or to be directed by opinion polls or by popular pressures into courses which they know to be wrong.

One of the best servants that a democracy has ever had, it seems to me, was Edmund Burke. It is worth recalling once again what he said to his electors at the Guildhall in Bristol, when they sought in midterm to harness him to their opinion on individual issues:

". . . I did not obey your instructions. No. I conformed to the instructions of truth and Nature, and maintained your interest, against your opinions, with a constancy that became me. A representative worthy of you ought to be a person of stability. I am to look, indeed, to your opinions—but to such opinions as you and I *must* have five years hence. I was not to look to the flash of the day. I knew that you chose me, in my place, along with others, to be a pillar of the state, and not a weathercock on the top of the edifice, exalted for my levity and versatility, and of no use but to indicate the shiftings of every fashionable gale."

That was in 1780. His electors had already been given notice six years earlier of his conception—I submit a sound one—of his duty as a Member of Parliament. Listen to this:

"Certainly, Gentlemen, it ought to be the happiness and glory of a representative to live in the strictest union, the closest correspondence, and the most unreserved communication with his constituents. Their wishes ought to have great weight with him; their opinions high respect; their business unremitted attention. It is his duty to sacrifice his repose, his pleasure, his satisfactions, to theirs—and above all, ever, and in all cases, to prefer their interest to his own.

"But his unbiased opinion, his mature judgment, his enlightened conscience, he ought not to sacrifice to you, to any man, or to any set of men living. These he does not derive from your pleasure—no, nor from the laws and the Constitution. They are a trust from Providence, for the abuse of which he is deeply answerable. Your representative owes you, not his industry only, but his judgment; and he betrays, instead of serving you, if he sacrifices it to your opinion."

Burke certainly disagreed with the theory that members of the legislature should consider themselves merely agents of their electors, bound to echo local prejudices or to vote in response to pressure from a lobby of local interests. He unhesitatingly told his constituents:

". . . Parliament is a deliberative assembly of *one* nation, with *one* interest, that of the whole—where not local purposes, not local prejudices, ought to guide, but the general good, resulting from the general reason of the whole. You choose a member, indeed; but when you have chosen him, he is not member of Bristol, but he is a member of *Parliament*. If the local constituent should have an interest or should form an hasty opinion evidently opposite to the real good of the rest of the community, the member for that place ought to be as far as any other from any endeavour to give it effect."

This may sound, in 1955, like a counsel of perfection. Yet Burke's words were merely a prescription of what has always been essential for the political health of any democratic society. Its basic ingredient is, and always will be, not so much political form or constitutional structure, as the character of individuals. What Burke told his electors was put more briefly by an American who asserted "I'd rather be right than be President."

In emphasizing that the determining factor in making democracy work is the character of individual men, I do not of course mean to minimize the value of constitutional devices and political institutions. One of the values of such institutions is precisely that they crystallize and embody the political insights of the past and thus help to transmit to the future the wisdom, restraint, and character of former generations.

Personally I believe, for example, that we in Canada have an advantage, as compared with most other democracies, in our monarchy. The distinction between The Queen, as Head of the State who does not rule, and the Prime Minister as Head of the Government which does, makes it easy for people to distinguish between the majesty of Government as such, and the activities of particular governments which are not always majestic. The monarchy represents and dramatizes, to an extent that no symbol that is less than human could do, the totality and continuity of the whole people, past, present, and future. It reminds men that in serving the State they must serve something more than the individual electors of the moment.

Again, it is my own view—and, of course, I am prejudiced in this matter—that our parliamentary system, with a Cabinet made up of men who are members of, and responsible to, the legislature, has certain advantages over the American congressional system. For one thing, the parliamentary method of responsible government means that the Cabinet, which has to submit from time to time to the chastening ordeal of election, is closer to the legislature than any non-elected ministers can normally expect to be.

Also, in our system, dissolution of Parliament and an election takes place if the government loses a vote of confidence. This makes the individual Member of Parliament more susceptible to party solidarity and less to short-run local pressures from special interests. He retains the power, with a majority of his fellow members, to overturn the government at any time, but at the price of a general election.

In this sense, the members of the Canadian or British House of Commons, of course, have more political power than United States Congressmen or Senators who, unless they resort to the drastic action of impeachment, are unable to remove the Executive between fixed electoral periods. On the other hand in our Parliamentary system individual legislators have a healthier respect for party unity because the price of weakening it is always the possibility of an election with all its uncertainty, personal and political. This gives considerable authority to the Executive, some would say too much authority. It also provides, in my view, reciprocal safeguards against serious abuse by either the legislative or executive power.

Whatever the relative merits of its various forms, experience during the past thirty years has shown major instances when *all* types of democracy have shirked commitments and refused to make the hard, necessary decisions which the situation required. On the other hand, since 1947 most of the great democracies, and notable among them the most powerful of all, the United States of America, have assumed responsibilities and accepted burdens unprecedented in time of peace.

The essential point to grasp is that there exists for democracies in world politics a set of issues which does not change with and is not determined by external situations, and which has little to do with diplomatic methods or constitutional procedures. This is what I might call the climate, the character, the moral basis, of our society. It would be foolish to say that our future in world politics depends exclusively on ourselves, for we are not alone. But it seems to me beyond question that that future, in foreign policy as elsewhere, will depend to a much greater extent on this internal factor than on anything else—on our quality as peoples, on what we believe in, and on what we really stand for.

The more I see of the policies and processes of government, the more remarkable it seems to me that serious and intelligent men could ever have brought themselves to propound or to accept the doctrine of historical determinism in any of its forms: the suggestion that we are slaves of fate and playthings of destiny. Such a view is only comprehensible when the human intellect loses its moral bearings.

Such a surrender is, of course, the essence of all theories of determinism. It not only blurs but blots out the whole question. For precisely what gives significance to life and history and politics is the possibility which men and nations always possess, though they by no means always use it, of acting creatively in their environment rather than merely reacting to it. To some extent, of course, all men transmit to the future impulses determined by the conditioning of the past, or respond almost mechanically to impulses from outside. But men can do more than this. If they will, they can always in some degree transform the situation in which they find themselves. They can take creative action which, while tailormade, as it were, to fit the environment, is in no sense merely a product of it.

The whole of our belief in the possibility of constructive action, whether by men or nations, is of course based on the assumption that man, and his mind, are more than merely products of heredity and environment, that he does have this possibility of contact with the unconditioned realm of the spirit. Public opinion and political judgment, therefore, are bound to reflect among other things the level of a people's moral insight and spiritual stature. This is as true in international as in domestic affairs.

I have often heard it said, as I am sure you have, and particularly regarding foreign policies, that governments pursue their national interest irrespective of moral considerations. This verdict, I think, begs most of the real questions. Of course governments pursue the national interest as they conceive it. That is their duty. The real questions are, however, first, how accurately governments (or people) can discern what is the real national interest, and second, how wisely they act in trying to reach the goals which they set. But here moral, even more than political, insight is required to decide where your real interest lies, and how to achieve it.

The foreign policy of a democracy is thus in large part a product and a test of the moral insight of a whole people.

In stressing the decisive relation of moral considerations to effective judgment—in international affairs as in other fields of activity—I am not, of course, suggesting that all political and diplomatic questions should be regarded as issues between right and wrong. Far from it. A moral approach to problems does not require that we should see all of them in simple terms of challenges to righteousness, or of black and white.

Indeed the contrary is true, and gray is the prevailing shade. This should induce humility and tolerance. Some wise words on this subject were spoken by Professor Brebner, whom I have already quoted, at the Columbia University bicentennial convocation on October 30, 1954. He said:

"During recent years, a hurricane of investigations and persecutions has lashed those parts of the earth where men in political authority have conceived themselves to be compelled to maintain one set of values and to attack all others. Throughout these operations, nothing has been more dreadful than the common assumption that every man must at all times be 'right.' Surely this intolerance of variation is the insolent vain-glory and self-assurance that the Greeks denominated *hubris,* the basic, the suicidal sin. In our time this sin may take the form of worshipping the power over nature or over human nature, or the deification of a man, an economic entity, a political party or a nation state."

An arrogant Pharisaism and smug satisfaction with one's own superior righteousness, in a person or in a nation, are not only unamiable qualities, they are not conducive to clear political judgment. The man whose humility and moral sensitivity is *least* highly developed is most likely to confuse principle with questions of fact or expediency, and to make an easy subconscious identification of his own viewpoint with the cause of right.

Furthermore, self-righteousness in international affairs is likely to lead to rigidity of thought and intolerance of other views. This often prevents a wise understanding of complex and changing situations, and tends to make diplomacy captive and inflexible.

We will need this wise understanding in our vigorous and unceasing effort to transform such improvement as has recently taken place into real progress towards peace. We should be prudent without losing our vision. President Eisenhower put it well and succinctly when he said that we should keep our feet on the ground and our heads in the stars. It is, of course, not easy to do this: to keep one's feet on the ground without getting stuck in the mud, or to keep one's head in the stars without drifting aimlessly in the stratosphere.

While exploring every possible step toward a genuine peace, we must be careful that we do not in the process prematurely weaken our defensive strength or weary in that vigilance which is still an essential part of the price of liberty. In his Easter message in 1954 Pope Pius said,

> "The danger of today is the weariness
>   that afflicts the good."

The world is still an unsafe place for the weary—as well as for the weak and unwary.

Nevertheless, strength and prudence without vision would be a sterile and unrewarding thing. To anyone educated in the rich tradition of our heritage it should be a truism that the real driving force of every important political and social movement has been vision.

When societies disintegrate—as several societies, European and Asian, have disintegrated during the past forty years under totalitarian pressure—the real explanation is that pointed out long ago by a Hebrew prophet: "Where there is no vision the people perish." We are far too apt to pigeonhole this in our minds as a moral exhortation rather than to recog-

nize it for the hardheaded political observation that
it is.

If this is true, then the greatest danger to our
civilization today lies not outside, but within. Professor Halle has put this very well in his recent book
Civilization and Foreign Policy when he says:

"If our own civilization remained in full possession of the vision on which it depends, the ideological challenge of communism would be quix-
otic. It could not endanger any more than termites
can endanger living wood. The danger to our civilization today comes from within, from the weakening of its vision."

It is, I think, clear that during the first four decades of this century the vision of Western society
was weakened. The results are apparent enough to
anyone who will take the trouble to reflect honestly
on the history of our times.

But the deepest tradition of our civilization is precisely the capacity for creative response and renewal.
It is possible, and may indeed be probable, that the
trend has now turned, that man may be moving,
even if somewhat unsteadily, toward a rebirth.
We cannot afford much unsteadiness in the nuclear
era, of course. But it is, I think, reasonable to believe that within democratic society during the past
few years progress has on the whole been in the
right direction.

If today we are justified in being cautiously optimistic, one ground for this lies, I think, in the very scale and profundity of the challenges which face us.

One advantage from external threats, as any good historian will point out, is that they may be used to prompt constructive responses, that they may lead to efforts and achievements which were in any case desirable but which, without the pressure from outside, men would have been too indolent or too short-sighted to undertake. Such pressure may thus sometimes be recognized later as an asset, leading to the development of habits and institutions of cooperation which remain to give men life and growth long after the challenge which impelled them has subsided or been destroyed.

The union in the 1760's of the thirteen American colonies, in reaction against pressure from Britain, is one example of this creative response. Confederation of the Canadian colonies a century later is another, prompted as it was to no small extent by fear of expansion from our powerful southern neighbours who at that time seemed to us flushed with visions of "manifest destiny" on a continental scale.

Certain recent examples also stand out. North American economic assistance after 1945 for the reconstruction of the democracies of Western Europe would, in any case, have been desirable, but it might not have been forthcoming on any adequate scale had it not been for the threat of Soviet imperialism in Eastern Europe.

In the development of North Atlantic cooperation in other fields, and in the habits of consultation to which it gives rise, there can without too much fancy be discerned a trend toward the revitalization of the old sense of community· of Western Christendom. These things may prove of use to men long after the defence needs of this generation have receded.

Similarly, cooperation between civilizations, including substantial economic and technical aid, while desirable in itself, is made easier of achievement by consciousness of external danger. If we survive the present tensions, it is, I think, not at all inconceivable that the contacts now being established under pressure may prove fruitful and constructive long after the external stimulus has disintegrated or subsided.

More important, however, than any other factor is, I repeat, the internal response; for a healthy society depends essentially on subjective factors, and the fundamental characteristics of a civilization are not institutions but how people feel, the way they think, above all the things they consider worth doing.

Life has always faced men with two fundamental questions: what to do, and how to do it. This is the age-old question of ends and means, always interdependent, always subject to derangement if priority is placed on methods rather than on the selection of goals.

"How?" is, of course, a technical question; and in all technical areas except the social sciences the West has, during the past half-century, produced triumphant answers. Indeed it is often suggested that the cure for most of our political and economic problems lies in putting behind the social sciences something of the same emphasis and energy and imagination that have paid off so strikingly in the natural science fields.

But there is, I think, more to it than this. What is really needed is rather to pay more attention to the primary question of goals: of *what* is worth doing.

This brings us into the field of values, where the emphasis is less on the mind than on the will, less on method than on the choice of ends. What is needed here—as I have already said—is vision accompanied by a hard-headed sense of reality. The two can and should go together.

The true realist is the man who sees things both as they are and as they can be. In every situation there is the possibility of improvement, in every life the hidden capacity for something better. True realism involves a dual vision, both sight and insight. To see only half the situation, either the actual or the possible, is to be not a realist but in blinkers. Of the two visions, the latter is the rarer, and the more important. But to be whole, and to be effective, we need both.

It is a fundamental principle of *all* the great religions of man, that values have objective existence —that they are, indeed, aspects of a reality which is universal and absolute. Recognition that these values can be only partially apprehended by individual men, only partially embodied in any particular piece of matter, only provisionally expressed in any given law or work of art, has taught us, or should have done, the necessity of tolerance and understanding.

Where erosion is at work, however, these qualities of tolerance relapse into indifference, into a lazy assumption that one view, one taste, one response is as good as another, with the corollary that none matters much. As a result, we sink into an uncritical acceptance of the shoddy and the second rate. This can be as great a danger as prejudice and intolerance, for it strikes at the very root of growth and healthy development.

I do not wish to close these lectures, however, on a note of pessimism or gloom. So may I return to where I began: to history, which provides a useful corrective to our worries and our present discontents and shows us that, while there is today great need for wisdom and resolution, there is no cause for defeatism or dismay.

Man, faced with the sad memories and the grim consequences of his failures to live peaceably with other men, has many times accepted as inevitable the prophecies of a doom that he has somehow managed to escape. Pessimistic speculation, or indeed *any* speculation, about the future is always a risky intellectual pursuit. In the eighteenth century the British Empire was considered lost beyond salvation at the dawn of its greatest hour. "I dare not marry; the future is so dark and unsettled," said William Wilberforce in 1790. Twenty-five years later, after Napoleon's new order had collapsed on the field of Waterloo as the old guard charged into the sunset and died, the confusion and turmoil seemed to many to presage total domination of Europe by the Czar's Muscovite hordes, whose presence aroused in the minds of Western Europeans emotions that have a familiar echo today. But in only a few years the Cossacks had retired to the Don, and Europe was given another chance to work out its salvation. Some thirty years later, on his deathbed in the midst of that enviable if somewhat stuffy era of calm and contentment which we have called Victorian, the great Duke of Wellington sighed, "I thank God that I am spared the ruin that is gathering around us."

The fact is that, to every challenge given by the threat of death and destruction, there has always been the response from free men, "It shall not be." By these responses man has not only saved himself, but has ensured his future.

May it be so again this time, as we face the awful and the glorious possibilities of the nuclear age.